Emotional Intelligence Mastery (EQ)

The Guide to Mastering Emotions and Why It Can Matter More Than IQ

By: Daniel Evans and Robert Goleman

Table of Contents

INTRODUCTION ---------------------------------- **I**

CHAPTER 1: WHAT ARE EMOTIONS? --- **1**

WHAT IS AN EMOTION? --------------------------- 2
HOW ARE EMOTIONS PROCESSED AND
EXPERIENCED? ----------------------------------- 5
WHAT ARE EMOTIONS USED FOR? -------------- 10
WHAT MAKES AN EMOTION NEGATIVE OR
DESTRUCTIVE? ---------------------------------- 13

**CHAPTER 2: HOW EMOTIONS CAN
IMPACT YOU** ---------------------------------- **17**

YOUR RELATIONSHIPS -------------------------- 18
*How Emotions Impact Your Relationships
-- 19
An Example of Emotions Having a
Negative Impact* --------------------------- 20
*An Example of Emotions Having a
Positive Impact* ---------------------------- 24
YOUR DECISION-MAKING ---------------------- 26
*An Example of Emotions Having a
Negative Impact* --------------------------- 26
*An Example of Emotions Having a
Positive Impact* ---------------------------- 28
YOUR PRODUCTIVITY AND EFFICIENCY --------- 30
*An Example of Emotions Having a
Negative Impact* --------------------------- 31
*An Example of Emotions Having a
Positive Impact* ---------------------------- 34
YOUR LONG-TERM EMOTIONAL HEALTH ------ 36

*An Example of Emotions Having a
Negative Impact*------------------------------ *37*
*An Example of Emotions Having a
Positive Impact* ------------------------------*40*
YOUR PHYSICAL HEALTH ----------------------- 42
*An Example of Emotions Having a
Negative Impact*------------------------------ *43*
*An Example of Emotions Having a
Positive Impact* ------------------------------ *45*
THE OVERALL IMPACT --------------------------48

CHAPTER 3: WHY EMOTIONAL INTELLIGENCE (EQ) MATTERS--------- 50

WHY EQ IS MORE IMPORTANT THAN IQ ------ 51
EQ HAS A GREATER IMPACT ON YOUR SUCCESS THAN IQ --- 53
DELAYING GRATIFICATION INCREASES FUTURE SUCCESS -- 55
A HIGHER EQ LEADS TO HEALTHIER RELATIONSHIPS --------------------------------- 57
A HIGH EQ WILL IMPACT YOUR PHYSICAL HEALTH--- 59
A POOR EQ IS LINKED TO POOR BEHAVIOR---- 61

CHAPTER 4: WHAT ARE THE CHARACTERISTICS OF EQ? --------------- 64

WHAT DOES A HIGH EQ EVEN MEAN? --------65
A HIGH EQ IMPROVES YOUR SELF-AWARENESS
--68
A HIGH EQ IMPROVES YOUR SELF-REGULATION
--69
A HIGH EQ SUPPORTS YOU IN BECOMING MORE MOTIVATED ---------------------------------- 70
A HIGH EQ MAKES YOU MORE EMPATHETIC - 71
A HIGH EQ IMPROVES YOUR SOCIAL SKILLS -- 72

CHAPTER 5: HOW TO IDENTIFY YOUR OWN EMOTIONS ------------------------------74

CONSIDER WHAT YOUR PHYSICAL RESPONSE IS -- 77
START PUTTING A NAME TO YOUR FEELINGS -- 79
AVOID JUDGING YOUR EMOTIONS WHEN YOU FEEL THEM -------------------------------------- 81
TAKE SOME TIME TO SIT WITH YOUR EMOTIONS -- 82
CONSIDER WRITING THEM DOWN -------------- 84
CONSIDER TALKING IT OUT---------------------- 86
FIND A SONG THAT EXPRESSES YOUR FEELINGS -- 88
INCORPORATE DAILY REFLECTION INTO YOUR ROUTINE-- 89

CHAPTER 6: HOW TO MANAGE YOUR EMOTIONS ----------------------------------- 92

BE WILLING TO TUNE IN------------------------- 93
SPEND A MOMENT IN REFLECTION -------------- 95
GAIN SOME PERSPECTIVE, LOOK AT THE BIGGER PICTURE --- 97
ACCURATELY IDENTIFY THE EMOTION YOU ARE FEELING -------------------------------------- 100
EXPRESS YOUR EMOTIONS TO OTHERS ------ 102
EXPRESS YOUR EMOTIONS PRIVATELY -------- 105
MONITOR WHAT YOU ARE HEARING -------- 108
CONTROL THE SNOWBALLING EFFECT -------- 111
PAUSE FOR A MOMENT------------------------- 113
IF YOU NEED TO, STOP COMPLETELY --------- 115
DISCONNECT FROM THE OUTSIDE WORLD ---- 117

CHAPTER 7: MANAGING OTHER PEOPLE'S EMOTIONS --------------------- 120

CONSIDER HOW YOU MAY HAVE CONTRIBUTED -- 123
NOTICE THEIR BEHAVIOR ---------------------- 126
REMAIN CALM AND RESPECTFUL NO MATTER WHAT-- 127

Respond with a Reflecting Statement --129
Ask Them Questions --------------------------132
Bring Movement into the Conversation 134
Encourage Them to Share Their Perspective ------------------------------------136
Identify What Matters to Them ----------138
Excuse Yourself from the Conversation -- 140
Apologize If You Need To -------------------142

CHAPTER 8: USING YOUR EQ TO BUILD HEALTHY RELATIONSHIPS ------------ 144

Building Healthy Relationships Feels Good ---145
Influencing Your Relationships with EQ --149
Becoming a More Supportive Friend ----- 153
Learning How to Contribute to Positive Emotions -------------------------------------- 155

CHAPTER 9: APPLYING EQ IN THE REAL WORLD -------------------------------- 158

Developing a Stronger Sense of Self ---- 159
Having Healthier Engagements with Strangers ------------------------------------- 161
Asking for Help More Effectively -------164
Actually Receiving Positive Solutions-- 167
Having a Healthier Network -------------169
Learning How to Fully Forgive and Move On -- 172
Reducing the Amount of Judgment You Pass -- 174
Discovering Ways That You Can Continue Learning -------------------------------------- 177

CHAPTER 10: EMBRACING YOUR EMOTIONAL JOURNEY -------------------- 180

REALIZE THAT YOU ARE NOT PERFECT ------- 181
CONTINUE PRACTICING EVERY SINGLE DAY --183
EMBRACE EACH EMOTION EQUALLY ----------185
DEVELOP A MINDFULNESS PRACTICE ---------187
SLOW DOWN WHEN YOU NEED TO -----------189

CONCLUSION -------------------------------- 193

Introduction

Congratulations on downloading *"Emotional Intelligence Mastery (EQ):* The Guide to Mastering Emotions and Why It Can Matter More Than IQ!"

As you read through this book you are going to be shown the many values of EQ, how it can help you change your life and ways that you can master it. Everything in this book is designed to show you how important EQ is and practical measures that you can take to begin raising your EQ and mastering it one day at a time.

EQ is a powerful skill that everyone can benefit from. Knowing how to manage your emotions and express yourself in an effective way is an essential skill for everyone to have. When you know how to effectively express yourself, you can enjoy many powerful benefits. Healthier relationships, improved emotional health, and reduced stress are just some of the many benefits that you can look forward to when you work on increasing your EQ.

In *Emotional Intelligence Mastery (EQ),* you will learn about what an emotion is, how it works, and how your body processes emotions. You are also going to discover the purpose of emotions including what their goal is and how you can use them effectively. Then, you will explore how your emotions impact you from a strictly primal perspective. This will help you understand where emotions come from, why they are so overpowering, and what results in most people not knowing how to effectively control their emotions.

In addition to learning about the primal aspects of emotions, you are also going to learn about important subjects such as the five characteristics of EQ and how you can improve them in your own life. You will also discover practical applications for EQ and how you can begin using these practical applications to improve your own. Through effective self-mastery and EQ mastery, you will begin to experience the many powerful benefits of EQ in your life.

As you read through this book, we encourage you to take your time and practice reflection and mindfulness. Allowing yourself to fully understand and process how EQ will impact you and how you can begin improving your own will ensure that you gain the maximum value from this book. The more you truly take the time to embrace each of these practices and master each one, the easier it will be to master your EQ overall.

We encourage you to purchase a journal that you can keep handy as you work towards mastering your EQ. Spending time reflecting on yourself and documenting your growth will show you just how far you have come. Furthermore, it will give you a clear understanding of where you can improve and how you can begin doing better each day.

Remember, the process of self-mastery is one that takes time and patience. There is no need to rush it or pressure yourself to master your EQ any faster than you feel is reasonable. Each person has their own stressors, traumas, and challenges to work through.

Giving yourself the space to work through each one as they come up will support you in complete healing so that you can do even better going forward.

If you are ready to begin the journey of self-development through the process of EQ mastery, please, begin reading! Remember, this is a personal journey for you to master your own emotions, so honor yourself no matter what comes up. And of course, enjoy!

Chapter 1: What Are Emotions?

Emotional intelligence, as defined by the Webster dictionary, is: "the capacity to be aware of, control, and express one's emotions, and to handle interpersonal relationships judiciously and empathetically." In order for you to understand what emotional intelligence (EQ) is and how it impacts your life, you need to understand what emotions truly are. This can support you in having a clear comprehension of what EQ is meant to impact and what it is that you are trying to gain or control when you learn to develop your EQ.

In this chapter, we are going to discuss the science behind emotions. You will learn what an emotion is, why we experience them, and how we use them in our lives. Chances are you have probably never considered how complex emotions actually are. The reality is they are quite deep. They also impact us in many ways especially when we are not consciously and purposefully controlling them.

What Is an Emotion?

The Webster dictionary defines emotions as being "a natural instinctive state of mind deriving from one's circumstances, mood, or relationships with others." It is also described as being an "instinctive or intuitive feeling as distinguished from reasoning or knowledge."

These two definitions teach us two important things about

emotions: they are malleable and influenced by external factors, and they do not necessarily need to be backed by a known cause or purpose. Instead, emotions are something that instinctively happens in response to what is going on around or within us.

Although emotions are an instinctive reaction that occurs within us, they are experienced in a very conscious manner. In other words, we are usually extremely aware of what emotions we are experiencing within us. When we take a conscious look at ourselves, we can generally state exactly what emotion(s) we are experiencing and how they are causing us to feel. In most instances, we can also pinpoint when the emotion was aroused even if we do not necessarily know why it was aroused.

Emotions themselves are quite complex. A lot of contradictory information exists on exactly what emotions are and how they are aroused within us. However, the most commonly accepted theory is that emotions are caused by the nervous system being aroused by various different circumstances. As this happens, various different states of arousal can occur causing the nervous system to determine which emotion is actually being felt by the individual. These emotions then adjust the psychological and physical responses in the person.

Some theories suggest that emotions are not necessarily the "end goal" of the nervous system. Instead, they are symptoms of the overall goal that the nervous system has. For example, if you feel angry, this anger is just one of the symptoms used by the nervous system to trigger a response that encourages you to protect yourself. The same general idea would be considered for all other emotions, too. Anxiety would be used to encourage you to flee a scary or dangerous situation, happiness would be used to encourage you to continue experiencing positive stimulation, and so forth.

How Are Emotions Processed and Experienced?

Emotions involve five different components. These include cognitive processes, subjective experience, instrumental behavior, expressive behavior, and psycho physiological changes. Each of these impacts how the emotion is experienced and processed by the body and mind depending on which emotion is being experienced.

For cognitive processes, your emotions will impact the way that you process information. This means that different emotions can influence your brain to be more receptive of different pieces of information. For example, if you are experiencing anxiety, your brain will look for any reason that it should be fearful or on the lookout for the danger that you need to run from. If you are experiencing anger, your brain will be looking out for the potential danger that it can fight against. If you are experiencing happiness, your brain will be looking for the positive stimulation and experiences in your environment.

Your subjective experience of emotions is the unique experience that *you* have with particular emotions. This is how you consciously recognize and process your emotions as an individual person. Because these are unique to you, your subjective experience is going to be different from others. For example, when you are experiencing anger, you may feel more fearful of your anger than someone else who is used to experiencing anger in a healthy manner.

Instrumental behaviors that you experience during emotions are the processes by which your body attempts to achieve a "goal." Essentially, when an emotion is experienced, a goal is also set out that the emotion is intended to reach. Fear, for example, is intended to protect you from a dangerous environment by keeping you consciously aware of what surrounds you or what could cause you pain. The instrumental behaviors you instinctively experience are your body's way of processing this emotion so that it is used to achieve its intended goal. Instrumental behaviors are often where emotions can "hijack" you and take over.

The expressive behaviors that you experience are how you *actually* process the emotions that are being felt. These are the actions that you take in order to enact the emotion that you are feeling. If you choose to laugh at something funny, for example, this is an expressive behavior. Likewise, if you choose to yell when you are angry, this is an expressive behavior. Essentially, anything you actually *do* rather than what you simply think about doing is an expressive behavior. Expressive behavior is where emotional intelligence really comes into play as it supports you in learning how to express your emotions in healthier and more effective ways.

The psychophysiological changes that you have when you are experiencing an emotion essentially refer to how your mind and body are literally changed whenever you experience an emotion. This explains how your hormone productions, physical posture, and organ functions change with varied emotions. For example, when you are stressed you experience an increase in cortisol and adrenaline production. This can also cause you to tense your muscles and can cause your organs to slow down their functions so that all of your energy and attention can be directed towards your stressors.

What Are Emotions Used For?

Although we all experience many emotions on a daily basis, very few people stop and wonder "why?" Some people may consider that we simply experience them because we are human. While this is partly true, it is also not. Emotions are experienced for a very specific purpose and they serve a very useful role in our ability to live and survive.

The simple ability to live and survive is not the only reason that we experience emotions, however. If you think about it, things like plants are capable of surviving and they do not experience or express emotions. Instead, our emotions are more closely linked to our ability to survive *as a part of the animal kingdom*. The emotions that we experience are intended to support us in staying alive and thriving as a part of a living system of organisms that fight, engage in intercourse, and hunt or gather as a means to survive. Beyond these basic forms of survival, humans have also evolved to become the most self-conscious animal to exist in the animal kingdom.

Like other animals, humans developed basic emotions as a way to survive under basic living conditions. Joy, fear, and stress were all designed as a way to support us in finding the necessary means to survive. As we continued evolving, however, we developed a complex rational system as well. This system is capable of supporting us in imagining our own past and future selves and experiencing reason. We are literally able to reason about our old selves and our future selves so that we can remember experiences we have had very specifically and change our future actions so as to avoid having those exact experiences, too. For example, instead of simply knowing that we need to run away from dangerous animals because they are a threat to our survival, we also learned that we did not want to experience this danger anymore. So, we creatively came up with a means to avoid these experiences in the future. An example of this is when we trap dangerous animals so that we could hunt them instead of being hunted by them. It was through the ability to reason that we were able to advance to where we are today.

However, our complex and evolved ability to reason has also lead to a change in our emotions. Because we can now remember things clearly and consider our future in a complex manner, we can experience emotions retrospectively or proactively. This is how we are able to recall past dangers and prevent future ones. It is also how many of us find ourselves feeling trapped in various emotions. For example, reliving past traumas through our emotions, or experiencing anxiety in regards to our future for fear of reliving past challenges. Although these emotions are intended to cause us to be able to protect ourselves and maintain our survival, they can also cause destruction if they are not managed properly.

What Makes an Emotion Negative or Destructive?

We have a tendency to loosely label emotions based on how we feel as we are experiencing them. Happiness, for example, is a good emotion because it brings pleasure when we feel it. Alternatively, sadness is considered a bad emotion because it brings us displeasure when we feel it. These two different labels do not accurately reflect what it is that we experience when we experience emotions, however. Instead, they merely reflect the level of pleasure that we experience alongside each emotion.

The true measure of what makes an emotion negative or destructive is in *how* it is experienced. In other words, it is a combination of our subjective experience and our expressed behaviors that make an emotion become negative or destructive. For example, if you are experiencing anger and you express yourself by becoming aggressive and ill-tempered towards another individual which causes pain, you have experienced a negative reaction of anger. This experience has become destructive because of how it was expressed. Your inability to express it effectively and respectively resulted in people feeling hurt, scared, or angry as well. This type of negative or destructive reaction can lead to broken relationships, painful arguments, or even full-blown physical fights depending on the severity to which the emotion was expressed. When you express your emotions in this way, you are typically expressing them in direct relation to your instrumental behaviors. In other words, you expressed your emotions in a very instinctual way. We call this "emotional hijacking" because your emotions essentially took over and you felt as though you had little control in the matter. As a result, you behaved in a way that you likely would not have had you rationalized the experience.

When emotions are experienced, understood, and expressed in a healthy manner, virtually no emotion is negative or destructive. This is because we are able to understand them, we can recognize their goal, and we can intentionally express ourselves in a way that reaches that goal without causing problems. Instead of anger resulting in a fight and a broken relationship,for example, it resulted in two people having a civil conversation and discovering a solution that served both people's needs. As a result, the anger still reached the goal it was produced to reach, but without being expressed in a way that was negative or destructive.

Chapter 2: How Emotions Can Impact You

Your emotions impact virtually every aspect of your life. From your ability to cultivate strong relationships to your ability to achieve your goals, everything you do is impacted by your emotions. Because your emotions play such a strong role in your behaviors and the way you express yourself, they truly do have a major power in your life.

It is important that you understand just how influential your emotions are in your life. In this chapter, we are going to show you how your emotions truly do impact your life. Each of the six sections below includes practical explanations as well as realistic scenarios that can help you personally relate to how emotions impact you. This will support you in seeing how much they truly can change your experience in all areas of your life.

Your Relationships

Possibly the biggest way that your emotions can impact your life is in your ability to make and maintain relationships with other people. Every other aspect of your life that is impacted by your emotions directly correlates to how you are able to build relationships with others. If your emotions are not being handled properly, it can have a detrimental impact on your ability to create and maintain relationships.

How Emotions Impact Your Relationships

People who have a low EQ have a tendency to have poor relationships in their lives. They may find themselves feeling lonely because they struggle to create or maintain relationships. They may also find themselves partaking in toxic relationships where the relationship is likely toxic towards both individuals in the relationship. This is because when emotions are expressed in a poor manner, people have a tendency to hurt each other more frequently. As a result, the relationship can become abusive or even traumatic towards one or both parties in the relationship.

Knowing how to effectively manage your emotions ensures that you are always expressing them in a way that is productive and not harmful to the other person. This eliminates the toxicity of your emotions and ensures that you are a positive and healthy person for other's to hang out with. This is an attractive quality for the relationship itself, as well as for other people. Most individuals will seek to hang out with someone who knows how to express themselves effectively so that their relationships remain positive and enjoyable.

An Example of Emotions Having a Negative Impact

Imagine that you are in a relationship where emotions are not being effectively expressed and so they have a negative impact on both parties. In this scenario, we are going to explore how emotions are negatively impacting two friends who have been friends for a long time.

"You arrive at your friend's house. You have been here many times in the past as the two of you are best friends. You know it well. You arrive and you realize your friend is feeling stressed because they have had a challenging day at work that day. Attempting to be a supportive friend, you ask them what is wrong. Your friend becomes agitated. Rather than expressing their desire to distract themselves with a more positive and enjoyable activity, they grow angry instead. Confused, you try and explain that you just want to support them. This quickly turns into an argument about how you never understand their needs and always push them to talk when they are not ready. At this point, you realize that they did not want to talk but it's too late, the argument has already started. Feelings are hurt and you are

both feeling angry and upset with each other. Rather than staying over and spending time together, you choose to leave early and call it a night. You leave with both of you feeling angry.

The next time the two of you communicate, it is awkward and uncomfortable. Mean things were said and you both felt the effects of hurt feelings. Instead of having the conversation in a positive and enjoyable way, it is spent apologizing to one another and attempting to retroactively resolve the argument that you both had."

Above, you witnessed what could happen if you or your friend did not know how to effectively express your stress and anger with each other. This type of experience is actually extremely common and happens all of the time between individuals and their loved ones, acquaintances, or even coworkers. Sometimes, it even happens between strangers. Not knowing how to effectively express your emotions can quickly result in more painful emotions becoming painful and challenging for everyone involved. The expression is rarely productive in reaching an effective goal and often results in people having hurt feelings. Sometimes, these types of emotions can lead to arguments that result in the relationship being permanently damaged. It is often these types of arguments that end long-time friendships and destroy families.

An Example of Emotions Having a Positive Impact

To show you how effective expressions of emotions can improve your experiences, let's take a look at the exact same situation being experienced between two people who have a higher EQ. You are about to see how an effective expression of emotions could have easily prevented the situation expressed above.

"You arrive at your friend's house. You have been here many times in the past as the two of you are best friends. You know it well. You arrive and you realize your friend is feeling stressed because they have had a challenging day at work that day. Attempting to be a supportive friend, you ask them what is wrong. Your friend

thanks you for attempting to support them but says that they do not want to talk about it. Instead, they would rather distract themselves with a fun evening together. You accept your friend's wishes and the two of you go on to share a fun night over dinner and a movie."

As you can see, someone's ability to effectively express their emotions can result in them being able to get their needs met. When people can identify their own needs and express themselves effectively, they often realize that their needs can easily be met without exaggerated or excessive actions. As a result, they can experience having their needs met and maintain a positive experience for everyone involved.

Your Decision-Making

Emotions have a powerful impact on your ability to make strong decisions in your life. Because emotions have the capacity to change how you perceive and process information, you can find yourself struggling to think rationally. As a result, the decisions that you make may be negatively impacted or hijacked by your emotional responses. This often happens when your expressed behaviors reflect your instrumental behaviors in a negative way.

An Example of Emotions Having a Negative Impact

In a negative experience, your emotions can result in your decision being one that has a negative outcome. This negative outcome could be one that has dangerous, painful, or unwanted consequences. An example of this is finding yourself at fault for a dangerous driving infraction, losing a friend because of your decisions, or losing your job. In the following example, I am going to show you how fear can result in you making irrational decisions that result in a negative outcome.

"You have a fear of dentists, so you refuse to go to the dentist. Every time someone tries to tell you to go, you grow angry and evasive about the subject. You refuse to go. Soon, your missed cleaning appointments result in a cavity. You can tell you have one because it hurts, but still, you refuse to go. If anything, your fear only grows because now you know that a basic cleaning has turned into a set of x-rays and a filling. You continue refusing until

the pain is so bad that you cannot bear it. Finally, you agree to go. The entire time you are there you are fearful and experiencing anxiety. The stress causes you to tense up and create even more pain resulting in the entire process being even more stressful. Because you waited so long, you had to get a root canal instead of a simple filling, meaning the process was more painful and lasted longer than it should have. The experience was far more traumatic and created even more fear for you because you put it off for so long."

An Example of Emotions Having a Positive Impact

Now, let's consider how your EQ could have changed your dentist experience. If you had you been able to recognize what the purpose of your fear was and express yourself effectively, you know you could have avoided a lot of added cost, time, and pain. Let's see how it could have gone differently:

"You have a fear of dentists, but you know that you need to go in for your semi-annual cleaning. Despite your fear, you book an appointment anyway because you do not want to miss your appointment. When you arrive at your appointment, you inform the dentist that you are fearful and that the experience makes you stressed out. The dentists hear your concerns and take the necessary action to make the experience less stressful for you. Because of their compassion and empathy, the experience was not as scary as you worried it would be. So, you leave the dentist feeling happy and knowing that

your teeth are healthy and cared for."

Your Productivity and Efficiency

Your emotions can have a huge impact on your ability to remain productive and efficient. When you are experiencing and expressing your emotions in a negative manner, you can find yourself feeling prolonged stress and resentment towards various experiences in your life. As a result, you may find it to be challenging for you to stay focused and take action when action needs to be taken. This can result in you struggling to get things done. In a localized experience, this can result in you performing poorly at work or not achieving your goals as quickly as you would like. In a more drastic experience, this can result in you achieving nothing at all and feeling chronic stress from falling so far behind. Alternatively, when expressed in a positive way, your emotions can support you in staying stress-free and focused. As a result, you are able to work without distractions and you get more done in the same amount of time. This way, your work does not take as long and you can move on to achieve more.

An Example of Emotions Having a Negative Impact

Let's take a look at how not knowing how to handle your emotions effectively can result in you not getting as much done. In this example, we are going to consider how a negative expression of emotions can result in a more localized experience snowballing and having a larger impact on your entire life.

"You find yourself feeling stressed out because a deadline is fast approaching at work and you have not achieved as much as you hoped that you would. Instead of being able to focus and get the work done, you find yourself getting distracted. You worry about how this could impact your entire life. If you do not get this done, your boss will be upset with you and this could result in an argument. You worry that in the future your boss will assign these tasks to someone else which could result in you not getting the promotion that you have been hoping for.

Now, rather than getting focused and completing your work, you grow even more distracted. Your focus dwindles as you begin getting sucked into your stress. Because nothing has gotten done, your stress grows even more. When you are off, you go home and the stress follows you. It results in an argument with your spouse, a burnt dinner, and going to bed feeling angry. When you wake up, you are even more stressed than you were the day before. So, once again you are not productive in reaching your goal at work. Now, this has resulted in you not being able to focus on anything. You know you have personal and professional goals that you want to achieve but you cannot seem to motivate yourself to achieve them because you are so stressed out by your experiences. The more you fall behind, the greater your stress grows. It is a no win situation that you cannot seem to escape from."

An Example of Emotions Having a Positive Impact

When you are effectively able to control your emotions, the snowball effect does not happen. This is because you both understand the emotion and know how to manage it so that it does not escalate. As a result, you are able to prevent one localized experience of stress from becoming an entire life filled with stress. This can ensure that you are able to stay focused and productive so that you can continue working towards achieving your goals.

If you were able to better handle your emotions, here is how the aforementioned experience likely would have gone instead:

"You find yourself feeling stressed out because a deadline is fast approaching at work and you have not achieved as much as you hoped that you would. Instead of being able to focus and get the work done, you find yourself getting distracted. You know that anytime you are stressed, you tend to grow distracted by your worries. So, you make a plan to overcome your fear and stay focused so that you can continue working toward achieving your goal.

You start by writing down everything that you are worried about. Then, you consider which of those worries is actually realistic. Next, you consider how your current actions are resulting in these worries potentially coming true. You realize that if you were to stay focused and get more work done each day, you could finish your project. Then, none of these worries would come true. So, you make a plan for how you are going to achieve more work and get the project done on time. After the plan is made, you immediately get to work on achieving each step in a timely manner. That way, your project is completed on time and none of your worries come true because the work got done."

Your Long-Term Emotional Health

Not being able to manage your emotions over a long period of time can have a significant impact on your emotional wellbeing. Studies have shown that mental illnesses such as depression and anxiety arise from chronically experiencing negative emotional expressions. While EQ may not singlehandedly support you in overcoming any mental health concerns you may be experiencing, it can have a powerful impact on supporting you in overcoming them.

An Example of Emotions Having a Negative Impact

In the following example, we are going to reflect on how one person's emotional expressions resulted in them having a negative long-term experience in their emotional health. This is a very common experience that people have and you may be able to relate to it to some degree in your own life.

"It started when you grew worried about a conversation that you needed to have with your boss. Even though it turned out to

be okay, you spent so much time worrying that it resulted in you not being able to get your work done. Then, you worried that this would get you in trouble. You went home feeling worried and you found yourself feeling irritable, too. So, when your spouse asked you a simple question, you overreacted and got into an argument. Then, you worried that this argument would not be able to be fixed. You went to bed worried about your work and your relationship.

As time went on, the worry grew. More time spent worrying resulted in less time spent working which meant you were at greater risk of getting in trouble or losing your job. This meant that you went home more irritated every day, so you experienced greater troubles in your relationship. As a result, you were also very worried about losing your relationship.

The experience continued to the point where it felt like all you could do was worry. Now, rather than simply worrying about something basic, you were worried about everything. You are worried about whether or not you would make it work on time, whether or not you had the money to pay for gas, or whether or not that rash on your arm was something serious. You worried about how people thought of you and what they thought of you and how they would treat you. Everything seemed to create more reasons to worry in your life. Before you knew it, your worry grew more severe. A simple concern would become a full-blown panic attack. You felt that you could not experience anything more than worry any longer and now you constantly worried that this worry would bring on another panic attack or something worse. Now, you were experiencing chronic anxiety."

An Example of Emotions Having a Positive Impact

If you were better able to control your emotions, mental health issues that resulted from chronic negative emotional expressions could be avoided. This does not necessarily mean that EQ is a sure way to fix every mental illness but it can be a strong support. In the following situation, we are going to look at how that worry may have been better expressed so that it did not snowball into a bigger and more complex emotional concern.

"Your worry started when you grew worried about a conversation that you needed to have with your boss. Even though it turned out to be okay, you spent so much time worrying that it resulted in you not being able to get your work done. Then, you worried that this would get you in trouble. Realizing that this had set you back, you decided to take a few minutes to release this worry from your mind. You spent a few moments grounding yourself and gaining perspective on your worries. Then, with a more relaxed frame of mind, you went back to work. You managed to get plenty done and made a plan to catch up on the rest the next day. You went home in a positive mood and woke up feeling great the next day. Everything you needed to accomplish was finished and the problem was resolved. You felt peaceful and confident in your decisions and actions."

Your Physical Health

The constant negative expression of emotions can have a severe impact on the amount of stress that you feel in your body. Stress does not always manifest as worry and anxiety. Instead, any time you feel an intense amount of any emotion and express it negatively, it can result in that emotion growing more powerful. Then, your body begins to produce cortisol and adrenaline. As a result, your stress increases whether you realize it or not.

The constant chronic exposure to hormones such as cortisol and adrenaline can result in negative consequences to your physical health. Many of these are annoying symptoms that we experience but that goes away when we relax. Others can be serious or even fatal. Another way that you can experience a negative impact on your physical health from your emotions is if you make a poor decision that results in you becoming hurt or injured. An example of this is when you drive too fast and get in a car accident. If you are not careful, your emotions can have serious negative consequences on your physical health.

An Example of Emotions Having a Negative Impact

In this example, we are going to explore how constant anger can result in someone having a negative experience in their health. This will show you how continually expressing yourself in unhealthy ways truly can have a physical impact on you.

"You cannot remember exactly when it started but as far as you know you have always been an angry person. Whenever people did something that upset or frustrated you, you would respond with serious anger. Often, something that could have been quickly resolved would instead turn into a major argument with you. This constant state of anger brought on a great deal of stress for you. The anger itself was stressful but you also felt greater stress from the side-effects of your anger. Every time you hurt someone else's feelings, lost another friend or broke something else, you felt more stress in your life.

Eventually, the stress began manifesting in physical symptoms. Your constant tension leads to headaches, muscle aches, and joint pains. One time, your anger got so bad that whilst breaking something you also hurt your wrist. You have suffered from countless negative physical symptoms from your anger, yet still, you remain stressed out and angry."

An Example of Emotions Having a Positive Impact

The positive alternative to having a high EQ is that you will not experience physical symptoms of stress because you are effectively self-regulating your emotions. As a result, your general stress levels are lower and you are able to carry on in life without any negative manifestations of stress.

However, for the sake of exploration and discovery, let's say you do experience a higher level of stress despite having a strong EQ.

Perhaps work has been particularly tough lately so you have been carrying a great deal of stress around with you. As a result, you are noticing that you are experiencing more headaches than usual and your body seems to ache in general.

If you responded in a healthy emotional manner, it would likely look something like this:

"You have been more irritable than usual because work has been particularly challenging. Your boss has been pushing you to get things done sooner because their boss was pressing for better results from your firm. The stress was building up and you were starting to feel angry. You also noticed that you were starting to get more headaches and your body was aching more regularly.

The other day in a meeting you realized that your fists were clenched even though there was no active reason for you to be stressed or angry.

After the onset of your third headache in two days, you realize that your emotions are not in check. So, you take a few minutes to explore how you are feeling. You write down your emotions and consider why you are feeling so angry. You realize that it is because your boss has been extra pushy lately. You spend a few minutes empathizing with them and realizing that they are also stressed and that they are simply trying to please their bosses so that things can calm down again. Instead of growing angry or getting more frustrated, you make a plan for how you can work more efficiently and get more done. You know that the extra work will impress your boss and keep them from being so pushy toward you. As your plan begins to work your stress lessens and you find yourself handling things more effectively again."

The Overall Impact

As you can see, your emotions can have a massive impact on how you experience life. When they are being negatively expressed, your emotions can cost you relationships, joy, and even your own health. This is obviously a very high price to pay for emotional reactions that you have when it comes to experiences that are challenging.

Many people falsely believe that there is nothing that can be done about negative emotional experiences. However, this is untrue. In fact, a lot can be done.

By working towards achieving a higher EQ, you can learn how to effectively express your emotions. As a result, your emotional experiences can lead to you having a more positive and effective impact at achieving your desired results such as having your needs met.

When you know how to self-regulate your emotions and express them in a positive way, everything changes. You are able to preserve relationships by effectively expressing yourself, you can make better decisions and your long-term mental and physical health is not atrisk of experiencing any negative repercussions. You stand to gain a lot when you stop paying the high price of a low EQ.

Chapter 3: Why Emotional Intelligence (EQ) Matters

Before the 2013 season, Chip Kelly took over as the head coach of the Philadelphia Eagles. Following his successful run in college, he was perceived as one of the best coaches in the league. Less than three years later, Kelly's lack of emotional intelligence resulted in him being fired from the position. He was fired with just one game left in the season.

This very same experience has happened to countless coaches and other famous sports individuals. It has also happened to many average people. Many times, people who are fired are fired because of their low EQ. #

This doesn't just happen with careers, either. Many relationships, including romantic relationships and friendships, have been destroyed by a low EQ. Not knowing how to effectively regulate and express your emotions can have a seriously negative impact on your ability to maintain healthy relationships with those around you. As a result, people don't necessarily want to be around you anymore. In the end, you are the one that loses out. In many cases, it's all because of a low EQ.

Why EQ Is More Important Than IQ

In the past, IQ was believed to be the most important thing. People sought after individuals who were the most qualified or the most intelligent. Bosses and CEOs wanted individuals with the highest credentials and the best titles under their names. Potential partners and friends wanted individuals who had the right personality and the status that came with being smart and well-educated. People were highly praised for having a high IQ.

It wasn't long, however, before people realized that just because someone had an IQ did not necessarily mean that they were the most qualified person for the job. In fact, a higher intelligence index did not necessarily mean that they were more qualified for *anything*. The real deciding factor was actually linked to EQ, not IQ.

EQ Has a Greater Impact on Your Success Than IQ

Although IQ is an important factor in helping qualify individuals for various different careers or professional pathways, it only accounts for approximately 20% of a person's overall success. Studies have shown that if you have a high IQ but a low EQ, chances are you are not going to be able to land and maintain a job or get too far in your chosen career. This is because people who have a lower EQ struggle to effectively build relationships with others. In other words, they're not likely to be a people person.

This inability to create and maintain relationships within the workplace, or operate in a professional manner at all, results in them having significant struggles when it comes to generating success. No matter how intelligent you are, if you cannot work nicely with the others in your industry you are going to struggle to get ahead. People want someone who is both intelligent and capable of presenting that information in a way that is kind and respectful toward others. They also want to hire a person who is more likely to contribute to having a healthy and enjoyable workplace culture versus someone who is incredibly smart but has volatile emotions.

Bosses actually prefer a higher EQ so much that they will happily take someone with a lower IQ but a higher EQ to fulfill a position. This is because they trust that this person will be able to fit well into the workplace environment. They also know that you can easily teach people how to do their job better but teaching someone to handle or manage their emotions is not nearly as realistic. Furthermore, it is not your bosses' job to teach you how to manage your own emotions. This is something that you need to be willing to do for yourself on your own time.

Delaying Gratification Increases Future Success

People who have a lower EQ have a tendency to struggle to delay their gratification. Instead, they prefer instant gratification that leads to them feeling good right now. In most cases, even if they know better, they will choose instant gratification and future suffering over delayed gratification with future success. This means that people who have a lower EQ can be very impulsive and unpredictable in their decision-making skills.

When someone has a higher EQ, they know how to handle and manage their emotions to increase their ability to delay gratification. As a result, they are able to maximize their chances of experiencing greater success in the future because they can remain committed to their goals and wait as long as they need to make them happen.

People who have a higher EQ have learned to go against mainstream society in a way that leads to their success. As a mainstream society, we have become highly addicted to instant gratification. Cell phones, fast food, credit cards, and our addiction to pleasure have all become more important to us than self-improvement. Anyone who actually takes the time to invest in self-development and improve their EQ is almost guaranteed to move far beyond the average crowd.

A Higher EQ Leads to Healthier Relationships

Our emotional skills directly impact the health of our relationships. As you have already learned in previous chapters, not knowing how to manage your emotions can lead to unnecessary arguments and toxicity in the relationships in your life. Understanding your feelings including what they are and where they come from, is imperative. This will support you in effectively expressing them so that you can communicate more effectively with others in your life.

When you can slow your own emotions down and think critically about them, you can also think critically about the emotions of others. While this does not mean that you should willingly endure toxic behaviors from others just because you "get it," it does mean that you will have a greater understanding of where they are coming from. As such, you can communicate more effectively with them in a way that honors your boundaries but considers where they are coming from.

Being able to have a strong EQ will also help you critically consider each relationship that you are navigating. As a result, you can adjust your expressions to effectively suit the needs of each relationship. For example, the way you express dissatisfaction towards your boss versus the way you express it towards your spouse will likely be two different things. With your boss, you need to approach them in a way that shows that you respect their authority and that you are not trying to deny or question it. With your spouse, you want to approach them in a way that shows that you recognize and respect them as your equal. Knowing how to adjust your emotional expressions based on the nature of each relationship is important.

A High EQ Will Impact Your Physical Health

Did you know that more than 80% of the health problems faced by society have in one way or another been linked back to the amount of stress that we experience? Stress can have a severely negative impact on our lives. Knowing how to manage your emotions effectively is going to help you decrease your stress so that your physical health does not struggle nearly as much.

The psychophysiological connection between your mind and your body is undeniable. Whenever you experience something mentally your body experiences something physically, too. For example, when you experience stress you tense up or when you experience the joy you loosen up. Knowing how to control your emotions allows you to control how your emotions are impacting your physical health. As a result, you subject yourself to fewer instances of negative psychophysiological repercussions.

A Poor EQ Is Linked to Poor Behavior

Studies have proven that there is a direct link between your EQ and your likelihood of committing a criminal act. This starts as early as childhood in children who are not taught to identify and express their emotions effectively. Often, they end up having a strong temper because they do not know how to express themselves. Instead of learning to interact with reason and conversational expression, these children learn to react instinctively. In other words, they react with their bodies often through aggressive acts of violence such as fighting. The inability to effectively identify and express their emotions results in poor social interactions which just leads them to have a difficult time making friends. This leads to them becoming a social outcast.

As they embrace this position as a social outcast, the attention they get from others is poor. They are either ignored or receive constant negative feedback for their actions and behaviors. This leads to even more feelings of frustration and anger, which results in even bigger acts of aggression. This continues to spiral until the child eventually learns how to manage their emotions if they ever do.

Children who struggle with a low EQ go on to struggle in school. They tend to find themselves hanging out with other children who experience the same struggles in their lives. As a result, the "gang mentality" can start. This result in them not only struggling to fit into society but they also no longer want to. Instead, they become hostile towards society. As a result, they end up finding themselves displaying acts of violence as a way to get "revenge" for what has happened to them in their lives.

Although family and environment both play incredibly strong roles in a child's likelihood of becoming a criminal, it is believed that this is because of how they impact a child's emotional well-being. Not having a positive role model and environment to develop healthy emotional skills in their lives results in children not knowing how to express themselves. As their negative emotions grow, their ability to express them lessen. Then, the child suffers and in many cases,society suffers alongside them.

Chapter 4: What Are the Characteristics of EQ?

As you begin to discover more about EQ and how it can change your life, you might also be wondering what exactly it is that you need to change in order to get there. Back in 1995, Daniel Goleman wrote a book on emotional intelligence that outlined 5 key characteristics that defined EQ. In this chapter, we are going to explore what these 5 characteristics are, how they relate to your emotions, and how they impact you in your life.

What Does a High EQ Even Mean?

After realizing that having a high EQ is, in most cases, more valuable than a high IQ, you might be wondering what it even means. What does it mean to have emotional intelligence and how can one get it? As we mentioned above, emotional intelligence is something that only you can teach yourself. You have to consciously decide that you want to improve your emotional intelligence and then you have to be willing to take action towards doing so. While people can equip you with the information that you need to teach yourself, no one can do it for you. You have to be the one willing to do it.

Having a high EQ means that your ability to regulate your

emotions is high. You have a greater sense of self-awareness, and therefore you can identify the emotions that you are experiencing. You also know how to identify when those emotions are being expressed in a negative way. Then, you can identify the signs that those emotions are coming and replace your typical expression with one that is more positive.

    Being able to regulate your emotions results in many wonderful benefits that can enrich your life. For example, when you can regulate your own emotions, you have the capacity to self-motivate a lot easier. Because you know how to adjust your emotions and the way you express them, you can use emotions like stress or excitement to motivate you into action. As a result, these emotions support you in achieving more rather than prevent you from achieving anything at all.

Another benefit that you gain from having a high EQ is that you can be more empathetic which actually significantly improves your social skills. Because you are able to become self-aware and understand yourself more intimately, you are able to understand other people's emotions better, too. As a result, you are able to slow down your own emotional responses to actually witness emotions in other people. As you do, you can empathize with them and regulate your own emotional responses in a way that shows empathy and compassion towards others. This leads to you having better social interactions which typically improve your chances of creating and maintaining relationships with others.

A High EQ Improves Your Self-Awareness

Emotional intelligence requires you to be able to actually know what emotions you are feeling at any given time. Although emotions are consciously experienced, you want to begin consciously expressing your emotions too. As a result, you need to regularly check in with yourself and become honest about what you are feeling and how it is affecting you. Through this, you begin to get to know yourself on a deeper level. Because you are checking in so frequently, you start learning about how different experiences impact you emotionally. You also start learning about your emotions and how you tend to express them. If you have a tendency to express them in a negative way, you can identify that and begin to pay attention to the signs of these experiences starting.

A High EQ Improves Your Self-Regulation

When you begin practicing the self-awareness that is required for you to improve your EQ, you start learning about what triggers your emotions and how they are typically expressed. As a result, you are able to begin practicing what is known as "self-regulation." This means that you can predict when different emotions are going to be sparked or feel when they are starting and you can actually intentionally slow down the process. That way, rather than becoming emotionally hijacked and expressing your emotions on an instinctive basis, you can express them purposefully. In other words, you can maintain rational thinking throughout the entire process of emotional expression and express yourself in a way that productively reaches your end goal.

A High EQ Supports You in Becoming More Motivated

Knowing how to tune into and regulate your emotions means that you can consciously avoid any distractions that may hold you back from achieving success. As a result, you can transform any emotion, from stress to anger, into one that motivates you. You learn how to take these emotions and discover what goal they are trying to achieve, then you can formulate a more productive and rational way to achieve that goal. For example, if you are stressed because a deadline is coming you can use that stress to formulate a plan and motivate you to work harder. This is more productive than becoming hijacked by your stress and worrying to the point that nothing gets accomplished.

A High EQ Makes You More Empathetic

When you are able to regulate your own emotions, you can also stop to consider how other people are feeling. As a result, you can consider how they may be influenced by their emotions and what feelings it may be causing within them. This means that you can actually adjust your own emotional expression to support the overall communication by considering the other person. For example, if you are a boss talking to an employee and the employee clearly seems intimidated by you, you can adjust your emotional expression to communicate in a less intimidating way. By increasing your friendliness and communicating your concerns in a kinder manner, you can reduce the intimidation factor and have a more constructive conversation with your employee.

A High EQ Improves Your Social Skills

As a result of your increased empathy and your ability to regulate your emotions to consider other people, your ability to have stronger social interactions is improved. This leads to you having an easier time creating and maintaining relationships with other people. Having a high EQ can actually improve people's attraction towards you because they trust that you will be able to regulate your emotions in a way that prevents or minimizes arguments and hurt feelings. Since your emotions do not lead to you being a toxic friend or person, they are more likely to want to have you in their presence. This can also lead to them actually having an improved ability to communicate and share with you. This is because they do not have to worry that you will have an unexpected or massive emotional reaction to something that they might say. Instead, if you disagree or feel angry towards something, you can express yourself in a kinder and more effective manner.

Chapter 5: How to Identify Your Own Emotions

One of the cornerstones in having positive mental and psychological health is the knowledge on how to communicate effectively. This is where the "talking cure" comes from. Essentially, it refers to understanding what your message is and effectively communicating it to other people. However, healthy communication does not start with your ability to speak clearly and your willingness to do so. Healthy communication actually starts with first understanding yourself enough that you clearly understand what it is that you want to say. This starts by understanding your emotions and knowing where they are coming from.

Your emotions play a massive navigational role in supporting you in understanding how you feel and what your stance is towards various subjects. The problem is most of us do not know how to accurately identify our emotions. This is because we have not been taught how to sit with ourselves and discover how we are actually feeling from moment to moment. As a result, we find ourselves feeling frustrated. This is because, when we do not know how to express ourselves, we grow angry. The need that the emotion we cannot identify is not being recognized and therefore it is going unfulfilled which leads to further frustration. Over time, this can grow to the point where you only ever recognize frustration but not the underlying emotion that is leading to the frustration.

In this chapter, we are going to explore how you can identify what emotions you are actually feeling. This is going to help you discover how you *actually* feel about things. You are going to learn how to dig past the feelings of stress and frustration and get down to the root of your emotions so that you can begin expressing yourself in a more accurate way. This is going to support you in having your needs met because now you will be accurately considering what they are and working towards fulfilling them, rather than ignoring them with anger.

Consider What Your Physical Response Is

Your physical response can be a great way to identify what it is that you are actually feeling inside. Physically, any time an emotion is triggered you will feel yourself change. This happens involuntarily as the process stems from your subconscious mind. When you take a moment to stop and reflect on your physical response, you give yourself the opportunity to begin looking for clues as to what your emotions might actually be.

Ideally, you should start by writing down what your physical responses are when they change between various emotions. At this point, you do not necessarily need to know exactly what emotion is triggering the response, you just need to identify when it happens. If you do begin sensing what the actual emotion is, or how it feels to you, write that down, too.

This process of stopping and reflecting is going to help you begin to recognize what your emotions are based on your physical response. If you are not entirely sure as to what to look for, consider these three areas of your body: your chest and shoulders, your stomach, and your face. In general, if your chest and shoulders become tense or tight, you are likely feeling some degree of fear or anxiety. If your stomach begins to feel tight or has a pain in it, you may be feeling sadness, distrust, betrayal or grief. If your face feels flushed like it is burning up, you may be feeling either embarrassment or happiness.

Start Putting a Name to Your Feelings

As you start noticing your physical responses and identifying when they change and what causes it, you can also start putting a name to your feelings. There are many different feelings beyond the basic ones that we tend to express. Taking the time to consider all of your feelings and what they might be can support you in getting a more accurate reflection of what your emotions truly are.

When it comes to actually putting a name to your feelings, start by identifying your physical response. Then, move on to assess your thoughts. What are you thinking about? Is it bringing you pleasure or displeasure? Use these clues to help you get a basic idea of what your emotion is. Then, you can easily use an emotional wheel to follow that emotion down to find our exactly what emotion you truly are feeling.

Getting a clear reflection on what exactly you are feeling is a good way to clarify your emotions. This is going to help you understand yourself and your emotional response deeper. As a result, you are going to have an easier time expressing this to other people. Instead of growing angry that you do not know exactly how you are feeling and therefore you do not know how to communicate yourself or your needs, you can communicate effectively. As you begin to practice, you will learn that it becomes even easier because you trust that through accurate reflection and communication you can have your needs met. In other words, your emotions become productive and serve the need that they were meant to serve.

Avoid Judging Your Emotions When You Feel Them

When you are feeling emotions, it can be easy to judge them as good or bad emotions. As you do so, you may also judge yourself based on how you think others will judge you for having those emotions. For example, if you are feeling jealous, you may fear telling your spouse of this because you do not want them to judge you for your emotions. This is extremely normal and many people experience it. However, in most cases, the judgment that you fear receiving is not a judgment that you would actually receive.

In the end, judging your own cmotions only results in you feeling a sense of inner conflict with yourself. Rather than being able to recognize, express, and work through your emotions, you add on an entire additional layer. Now, you also have to work through feelings of shame and guilt for feeling something that you believe is negative or a bad reflection on who you are. You also have to work through the fear of knowing that other people might also think of your emotions as "bad," which can make you reluctant to even express them in the first place. As a result, you may find yourself bottling your emotions up rather than effectively expressing them.

Take Some Time to Sit with Your Emotions

Spending some time actually sitting with your emotions is a powerful way to check in with yourself and how you are feeling. In many cases, when we do not slow down we find ourselves not adequately recognizing and expressing our emotional selves. The business of life and of our thoughts can overwhelm us and prevent us from actually tuning in and listening.

Spending just a few minutes each day checking in with yourself and asking yourself how you are doing is a great way to let any unexpressed or unrecognized emotions come to the surface. Then, you can check with these emotions and consider why they are being felt and what their purpose was. If there is anything that you need to do in order to express those emotions, you can then do so.

It is important that you truly make time to sit in stillness and listen to your emotions. Often, instead of actually sitting and feeling our emotions we distract ourselves. These days, common distractions include social media or cell phones. Instead of checking with ourselves and processing our emotions, we scroll social media or we play mindless games to keep ourselves distracted. As a result, we never recognize, identify, or express our emotions. This leads to them being bottled up and expressed later in an ineffective and unproductive manner.

Consider Writing Them Down

Writing is a powerful form of therapy and a wonderful way to express yourself. When you begin writing down your feelings, you move thoughts out of your mind. As a result, you begin getting your emotions flowing. This can lead to you following thought trails down to the root, finding out what caused your emotions, and what exact emotions were brought about.

As you write about your emotions, you will not only discover what they are and what triggered them but you will also give yourself the opportunity to express them. Any time you move emotions out by saying them or acknowledging them, you clear them out of your body and mind. If there is anything that you need to do to follow up on an emotion, you can acknowledge that need too and then create a plan to actually move them out. As a result, you are able to free up space in your thoughts and fully release the energy of each emotion.

A great way to use writing as an opportunity to recognize and express your emotions is to include a daily journaling practice in your life. Even if you are not much of a writer, just jotting down your thoughts in no particular order can be helpful. The only person who will ever look at this journal is you, so do not feel any pressure to do it the "right way." What you write will not be judged, so simply get it out!

Consider Talking It Out

Another excellent way to process your emotions and discover what you are feeling is to talk to someone else. You can talk to a trusted loved one or a professional who can spend time listening to you and hearing what it is that you have to say. As they listen to you, you have the opportunity to move your thoughts and emotions out and clear your mind. This means that you will have the opportunity to say and hear your thoughts being expressed out loud. This gives you a great opportunity to reflect on your own thoughts and emotions as you are speaking.

When you talk with someone else, you also get the unique opportunity to have them listen and reflect back to you. The other person can help you process your emotions, understand how you are feeling and recognize things that you may be overlooking in your own mind. As a result, you get the chance to look even deeper into each emotion and what is causing it. This helps you have a better ability to understand yourself on an emotional level. You can also use this as an opportunity to discover new ways to express your emotions that will be healthier and more effective.

Find a Song That Expresses Your Feelings

Music has a wildly powerful ability to help people identify and express their emotions. In many cases, music that we listen to accurately reflects how we are feeling inside or about ourselves. In other words, what we listen to tends to sound the way that we are feeling. If you are struggling to express your emotions, look for a song that expresses them for you. Spend some time listening to the song and seeing which parts of it you connect with the most. This can help you identify what it is that you are feeling yourself.

Using music as a way to identify your emotions is not only going to support you in actually clarifying what you are feeling but it will also support you in feeling a sense of being understood. The feeling of someone else understanding you creates a sense of compassion within you thereby helping you to realize that the emotions you are feeling are okay to feel. This can support you in overcoming self-judgment and feeling more at peace with what you are emotionally feeling in regards to your experiences. It can actually help you pave the way to expressing yourself with greater confidence and compassion towards yourself.

Incorporate Daily Reflection into Your Routine

There are going to be times where your emotions may get the best of you especially early on in your practice of developing your EQ. For this reason, incorporating a time for reflection into your daily routine can be extremely helpful. You can do this as you are journaling, after you have considered your present emotions, or you can do this separately through your thoughts.

Spending time reflecting on your day is going to help you identify what you felt was a success and what you felt could have been handled well. This way, you can begin creating new solutions for how you want to handle your emotions going forward. This is also a great time for you to identify any emotions that you may not have recognized as you were actively feeling themthroughout the day. You can take a few moments to put a name to the emotion and reflect on what it felt like to feel that emotion. That way, in the future, when you feel that emotion you can recognize it, identify it, and express it more effectively.

Just a brief five minutes of self-reflection each day can support you in identifying your emotions and understanding them on a greater level. This is an excellent way to begin practicing self-awareness and improving your self-development one day at a time.

Chapter 6: How to Manage Your Emotions

Once you are able to identify your emotions, you need to be able to effectively manage them. Managing your emotions is truly the key behind EQ. Knowing how to recognize your emotions and then manage them ensures that you can express them in a way that is productive. This also ensures that you do not carry emotions around with you, bottling them up until you have no choice but to express them. As a result, recognizing and processing emotions in the present moment becomes a lot easier because you are not attempting to express just one while still trying to hold back several others.

In this chapter, we are going to show you how you can work towards managing your own emotions both privately and in social settings. This is going to ensure that no matter where you are or what you are doing when you feel an emotion, you can recognize that emotion and process it appropriately.

Be Willing to Tune In

The first step in being able to actually manage your emotions is being willing to tune in. Having the capacity to recognize and understand your emotions is important but if you are not regularly tuning in then this doesn't necessarily matter. Your willingness to tune in to your emotions and needs every single time you witness an emotion coming up is essential.

Sometimes, you might not even recognize yourself avoiding your emotions or attempting to repress them. When you have grown so used to avoiding your emotions, repressing them just seems natural. You likely don't even recognize that it is happening. This is why, especially at first, a willingness to tune in and really listen is important.

As you are learning to tune in, a good way to bypass your habitual ignorance towards your emotions is to set reminders to tune in. Having a reminder on your phone that alerts you to stop and take an account of your emotions every hour will support you in actually remembering. Then, before you know it, stopping for self-check-ins will become a habit.

When you do check in, make a conscious effort to be extremely honest with yourself. Make sure that you are not tuning in just to continue to blatantly ignore the harder feelings. Take an honest account of all of them and how they are impacting you. This will ensure that no underlying emotions go unrecognized and, thus, get bottled up and become an issue.

Spend a Moment in Reflection

Once you identify that there is an emotion that needs to be addressed, spend some time reflecting on that emotion. You want to take the time to truly understand the emotion, including where it has come from and what it wants to achieve. This way, you know the purpose of the emotion and what exactly needs to be done to resolve it.

As you reflect, see if you can pinpoint when the emotion started and what was happening just before it did. This will help you begin to understand where that emotion is coming from. If you realize that the emotion stemmed from another emotion, for example,your agitation has stemmed from stress, and then go to the root of that emotion too. This will ensure that you completely understand where this emotional experience is coming from and what has caused it to get to the point where it is at now.

Taking this moment to reflect is going to support you in managing your present emotion as well as managing future experiences with this same emotion. This is because, as you reflect, you will begin to understand what causes this emotion to come up for you. In the immediate moment, you can use this understanding to communicate your feelings and needs and resolve the current emotion. In the future, you can use this understanding to help you identify what could possibly trigger the emotion so that you can begin dealing with it right away when it arises. That way, your emotions are less likely to become bottled up. Instead, you can process them the moment you begin experiencing them and then let them go completely.

Gain Some Perspective, Look at the Bigger Picture

After spending some time reflecting on the past and where

the emotion came from, you also want to spend some time reflecting on the future. Spend this time getting a look at the bigger picture. This is going to help you critically think about what specific outcome you want to achieve. For example, if you are upset with your spouse but you know that you love them and do not want to have a strained relationship with them, you can act accordingly. In this example, you know that you need to resolve your emotions in a way that does not negatively impact your future. Then, you can resolve them in a more complete and kind manner that results in you getting your needs met and your relationship staying healthy and intact.

In most experiences, our desire to have a negative outcome is slim. We rarely enter any emotional experience hoping for a negative outcome. Even if you do not like the other person and you want to terminate a friendship with them, chances are you do not want to experience long-term residual effects from the experience. Instead, you just want to end the relationship and move on.

You also need to think beyond that isolated person and event. Everything you do has consequences that you probably do not recognize when you are in the heat of the moment. These consequences could negatively impact your other relationships, your career, or even your overall stress levels. Knowing how to account for *everything* that could be impacted by your emotional expression can ensure that you keep this isolated event in perspective. Managing it effectively and without being mean or unkind to the other person can ensure that your needs are met and that you are not required to pay any excessive consequences for your excessive behaviors or actions.

Accurately Identify the Emotion You Are Feeling

Next, laser focus your attention on the exact emotion that you are feeling. Now that you have some perspective and a deeper understanding of how you got there, consider your emotions again. Are your emotions truly what you had originally thought they were or have you gained a deeper insight as to how you are actually feeling?

Spend a few moments considering your thoughts and the

feelings that you are having in your body. If you want to successfully express yourself, it is essential that you know exactly how you feel. There is nothing worse than believing that you are feeling one thing, effectively expressing that emotion, closing the situation, and then realizing that there was a completely separate emotion that was left unexpressed. This makes dealing with that separate unexpressed emotion much harder.

Spending just a few moments to check in with yourself once again and see how you are really feeling can ensure that you express yourself completely. That way, you can make sure that you are handling all of your emotions in that very moment and not holding on to any. Even if the emotions are challenging to express or admit to, it is essential that you do so if you want to completely work through them and move on.

Express Your Emotions to Others

Once you have a greater sense of what you are feeling, where it is coming from, and what you want to achieve, you need to begin expressing your emotions. In a situation where these emotions need to be expressed to someone else such as if they have contributed to you experiencing those emotions, you need to know how to express yourself.

There are certain things that you need to consider when it comes to expressing yourself to other people. For example, no matter what emotion you might be feeling and no matter how intensely, you need to ensure that you are expressing yourself compassionately and respectfully. Even if you are extremely outraged by another person or you do not necessarily like them, you need to treat them with manners.

Treating people poorly can have a negative impact on you. It can earn you the reputation of being someone who is emotionally volatile, unkind, or even a bully. Being unkind can result in you losing things such as friends or your job. It can also result in you feeling guilty and having even more emotions to process as a result of how you expressed yourself. This can lead to stress and many other emotional issues.

As you are speaking, make sure that you are taking your time and expressing your message in a complete manner. Explain everything that the other person needs to know to understand where you are coming from and what you are trying to achieve. This ensures that they hear everything and that they are completely aware of what is causing your emotional experience. If you hold anything back or do not express yourself completely, the other person can only respond to what they know. This can result in a thing being left out and you feeling as though your needs are unmet because you did not express yourself completely.

Finally, make sure that you are also considering how you are coming across in your tone of voice and body language. Just because you are speaking in a compassionate and kind manner does not mean that you are coming across that way. Choose both words and a tone of voice that expressesyou in a polite and respectful manner. Then, make sure that you are standing in a way that is still open and friendly even if you are not necessarily feeling that way. This will ensure that the other person understands that even though you are feeling emotional, you are willing to find a solution to those emotions. This keeps them more open to communicating and supports both of you in reaching a mutual resolution that brings the problem to a complete closure for both parties.

Express Your Emotions Privately

Sometimes, the emotions you experience are not ones that you feel that you can express to others. Or, maybe you don't need to. For example, if something happened during the day that triggered you to remember what it felt like to be bullied, you might find yourself feeling frustrated and upset. There may not be anyone to blame as the situation could have been completely innocent, yet resulted in an emotional reaction from you. In this case, the expression of your emotions is one that needs to be more personal rather than expressed to someone else. Here, you are healing an emotion from your past.

Expressing your emotions on your own truly requires you to spend some time in reflection and letting yourself feel heard and acknowledged. A great way to do to this is by spending time letting yourself think about how you are feeling and then actually feel it. For example, if you are feeling sad, cry. If you are feeling angry, do some cardio and let the energy move through you. If you are feeling scared, spend time validating that fear and sitting quietly with yourself. Do what you need to do in order to actively feel that emotion.

Once you have actively felt the emotion, move on to processing it and understanding it. This is how you are going to come to a resolution with yourself so that the emotion feels completely expressed and used. As a result, you experience closure. Journaling is an incredible way to express yourself in a way that moves the words out of you and helps your thoughts clear out. Keep writing until you feel as though you have completely worked through those thoughts and the emotion and then let yourself relax as you let the emotion itself resolve.

Monitor What You Are Hearing

When you are experiencing an emotion, many times you are experiencing many thoughts going along with that emotion. These thoughts that come from your own inner voice can really exaggerate your emotion if you are not careful. For example, if you are fearful, your thoughts may begin to spiral into an extreme state of worry until you find yourself completely anxious and struggling to return to a more neutral or relaxed state. When left unmanaged, thoughts can aggravate our emotions even further and result in us feeling them in a more extreme manner.

Listening to what is going on with your inner voice is extremely helpful. First, it can give you a better sense of what you are feeling and why. Typically, this inner voice is speaking in a way that clearly states your emotion. The content of what it is saying also directs you toward what you are feeling and what has caused it. By listening to that voice, you can identify your exact feelings and where they are taking you. You can also identify what it is that your emotion is trying to accomplish.

As you listen to this voice, also make sure that you keep it in perspective. In many situations where emotions are heated, we have a tendency to focus solely on our own narrative and ignore everyone else. We become so engaged in our own thoughts and needs that we completely forget to consider the other person. Make sure that when the other person is speaking and expressing themselves that you keep your own inner voices quiet. This can ensure that you are actually listening to the other person and understanding them. As a result, you are communicating with each other as opposed to both speaking at each other with no effective communication actually taking place.

It is also important that you keep your inner voice in check. Once you identify it and what it is telling you, do not let it spiral and take you completely out of control. Realize that many of the thoughts that it is having are based on fear or presumption of what is going to happen, not on what is actually happening in that very moment. Thank the voice for what it has offered you but make sure that you do not let it amplify your emotions in a way that causes them to take over. That way, your inner critic stays constructive rather than becoming destructive.

Control the Snowballing Effect

Emotions are well-known for spiraling. One emotion can quickly become a full-blown train of emotions if you are not careful. For example, if you are stressed, that stress can quickly become an irritation, which becomes a frustration,and later transform into anger and in turn can spiral all the way to rage sometimes. Likewise, if you are happy, you can become excited, then ecstatic, and so forth.

When your emotions spiral beyond your control, it can result in them completely taking over. Often,this affects your decision-making skillsand your expression turning negative. This is why when people are extremely happy they end up making decisions such as impulsive purchases that they later regret. This is an example of being hijacked by a positive emotion. We generally do not think of this to be a bad thing because it brings us pleasure but it can still have highly negative consequences.

Knowing how to keep your emotions in check can prevent this snowballing effect. You want to start by acknowledging what the emotion is and setting out to manage and express that emotion immediately. The longer emotions go unrecognized and unresolved, the more likely it is that they will snowball and result in other emotions being felt. In the end, you can easily be emotionally hijacked if you do not acknowledge your emotions and give them the attention they need right away.

Pause for a Moment

When you are looking to manage your emotions, take some time and pause. Just a few moments spent pausing can support you in quickly getting a handle on your emotions. Even if you simply wait for three breaths to pass and then you continue, this is plenty to slow the emotion down and give you the opportunity to actively manage it in action.

Pausing for a moment during emotional expressions is your best opportunity to make sure that you are practicing mindfulness while you express yourself. That way, you have the moment you need to reflect on your past and future, gain perspective, and proceed intentionally.

As you take this moment to pause, also quickly reflect on your physical self. Consider your posture, how you are carrying yourself, and if anything has changed in response to your emotions. Then, consciously and intentionally relax so that you can adjust your emotions from the outside in. This is a great way to cue your mind to take a break and calm down on its emotional outburst. Once you have begun the process of calming down, expressing yourself and engaging in healthy conversation with those around you becomes a lot easier.

If You Need To, Stop Completely

In some cases, the emotions you are experiencing can be extremely intense. No matter how many times you pause, you may find yourself still struggling to stay in control over your emotions. If it is a possibility, taking a break from the conversation is ideal. If you can only take a few minutes, take them. If you can take more, take it.

Taking the opportunity to have a complete break from the engagement and to walk away gives you a chance to ensure that you are not responding to your emotions in a way that you will later regret. Use this time apart to express your emotions privately to yourself as this will allow you to understand yourself and your needs more clearly. Then, spend some time completely relaxing and diffusing from the emotions that you are experiencing. That way, when you return to the conversation, you are in a calmer state of mind and you can express yourself more clearly and effectively.

The important part of breaking a conversation or engagement to avoid a negative emotional experience is that you have to make sure you both agree upon when you will come back to the conversation. Leaving an emotional conversation indefinitely can result in both parties growing in resentment and avoiding the conversation. As a result, more emotionarises and festers. This means that the next conversation if it ever happens, might be even more complicated than the first one. Having clear expectations and knowing when you are coming back ensures that you both get the break you need but that you also both get a resolution to the situation. This brings closure to it so that both parties can move on.

Disconnect from the Outside World

Each day you should spend some time disconnecting from the outside world. Incorporating this into your daily self-reflection routine is a great idea. The outside world has a tendency to stir emotions within us even if it did not intend to. As a result, we can find ourselves feeling an increase in stress, sadness, frustration, anxiety, and other emotions simply because of the world around us.

Our current generation is completely plugged in almost all of the time. This means that we are constantly consuming content that has us generating various different emotions. We can experience many emotions in a short period of time just from scrolling a social media feed or reading a newspaper. If we do not recognize, honor, and express each of these emotions, it can result in emotional overwhelm. This is why self-reflection and private expression is important.

It is also important to the emotional and psychological well-being that you disconnect on a regular basis. This will give you a sense of complete quiet and calm where no new emotions are being fed into your system. As a result, you can take somewhat of a break. This gives you the opportunity to "shut down" for a while and really experience complete freedom from any lingering emotions that may be keeping you feeling frustrated or even upset. This can actually contribute to the snowballing effect too.

Ideally, you want to spend at least an hour a day completely disconnected. This does not mean that you cannot do anything during that hour. Instead, it means that you can simply focus on what is directly in front of you and leave distractions out of it. For example, if you are cleaning the kitchen and then making dinner, avoid having your phone out or the TV on in the background. That way, you can enjoy being completely disconnected for approximately an hour. This will bring more peace to your mind and give you time to work through your thoughts rather than let them fester and turn into a snowball of emotions.

Chapter 7: Managing Other People's Emotions

Although you cannot control other people, you *can* control and adjust the way you respond to other people. As a result, you can actually use your own response to manage other people's emotions during conversations. This is a great way to take into account how the other person is feeling and how they are expressing their emotions. Then, you can use this information to discover what the best way is to get your needs met.

For example, if the other person is extremely sensitive and angry at that particular moment, you can communicate in a gentle yet firm way. This can support them in calming down while also expressing and asserting your needs.

Knowing how to manage other people's emotions during conversations is extremely important. This is how you can go from being someone who is decent at social interactions to someone who is incredible at them. People who are known as a "people person" tend to be great not only at managing themselves and their own emotions but also at managing other people's emotions too.

It is important to understand that when you are managing someone else's emotions, you are not actually taking responsibility for their emotions. You are also not taking the management of how they express themselves in as your own responsibility. Instead, you are simply adjusting your own emotional expression as a means to support them in managing theirs. When this is effective, it can support the other person in expressing themselves more effectively. In the end, your conversation is more productive.

If your conversational partner absolutely refuses to calm down, it is not your responsibility to take the blame for this. Because you cannot control how other people manage and express their emotions, if they absolutely refuse to respond to your attempts, that is their own problem. The goal here is to communicate in a way that considers them and has compassion for their emotions, not in a way that makes you personally responsible for their expression.

In this chapter, we are going to discuss how you can consider other people's emotions and manage them during conversations. In most situations, this will support both of you in more effectively managing your emotions and communicating more productively. As a result, both of you are able to get your needs met and no one has an emotional outburst that results in hurt feelings or awkward emotional situations.

Consider How You May Have Contributed

Whenever you are in a conversation where someone is getting emotional, consider how you may have contributed to that emotional response. Knowing how to take responsibility for your contributions can ensure that the dispute does not deteriorate to a process of discovering "who is to blame."

Typically, emotional responses symbolize that someone feels that their values have been violated. So, something has violated what was important to the other person. This something may have been you personally or it may have been something or someone else that they encountered prior to your conversation.

Often, a person's negative emotions have a tendency to mask what they are actually thinking or what thought process resulted in them reaching that emotional state. Spending some time reflecting on what was happening just moments before their emotions changed is a good way to consider how you may have contributed.

If you believe that you have contributed to their emotions, it is important that you also ask. Even though you may be able to find clues on your own, you will not know exactly how you may have contributed unless you straight out ask. In many cases, the other person's thoughts and emotions have been changing long before their actual expressions changed. For this reason, your assumption may be completely wrong.

Once you know how you may have contributed to someone else's emotions, you can start taking action. You can apologize if you need to, adjust the way that you are behaving or treating them, and express yourself in a way that is more considerate to their needs.

Notice Their Behavior

When emotions begin to come into play, it is not unusual for both parties to become so consumed by the content of the conversation that they fail to recognize emotions. When you are having a conversation with someone and you notice it starts to become emotional, spend some time paying attention to what is actually happening.

Look at the person's body language and consider what it is saying to you. Do they look angry and annoyed? Defensive and uncomfortable? Fearful and intimidated? What is going on with their tone of voice? What is going on with their face? Pay attention to the things that they are communicating without words.

People's body language, facial expressions, and tone of voice say a great deal about how they are feeling and what they are thinking in any given moment. When you learn to gauge these reactions, you can begin looking for ways to communicate that diffuses the situation. This can support you both in coming down from your emotional ladders and expressing yourselves more intentionally and effectively. As a result, your conversation can have a productive outcome that accommodates for both individuals emotions and needs.

Remain Calm and Respectful No Matter What

When you are having a conversation with someone, it is imperative that you remain calm no matter what. If you don't, you will find yourself adding to the gravity of the situation and escalating the emotional reactions rather than diffusing it. It is important that even if the other person's emotional intensity increases, yours needs to remain the same.

Typically, when someone's emotional intensity escalates beyond a certain point, their ability to reason is diminished. They struggle to think rationally and their decision-making skills are weakened. This means that they may begin to express themselves in an incredibly poor manner. Since the only person that you truly can control in any interaction is yourself, it is up to you to make sure that you stay calm and keep your emotions in check. When you can do that, you ensure that you are not escalating the situation. Instead, you can work towards diffusing it.

Controlling your emotional response will come from using the steps that you have learned in chapter 6, in regards to recognizing and expressing your emotions effectively,this way, you can continue to express your needs while also considering how the other person is feeling. The idea is not to become passive or passive-aggressive, but rather to consider your own emotions and choose the best course of action to express them and have your needs met.

Respond with a Reflecting Statement

When you are in the middle of an emotional conversation with someone else, using reflecting statements is a great way to show the other person how they look through your eyes. This is your opportunity to show that you are trying to listen and understand and to see if you truly have been. This also gives the other person the opportunity to discover whether or not you understand them properly. If you are not, they can better explain themselves so that you can understand more clearly.

Reflecting statements are essentially statements that you make that reiterates what the person is telling you in the way that you best understand it. For example, "What I'm hearing is..." or "I can see that you're feeling..."

When you use reflecting statements, you also validate the other person. This is a great chance to show them that you recognize how they are feeling and that you understand why they are feeling this way. It also shows that you want to work towards understanding them better so that you can discover a solution that supports both of your needs.

Avoid using reflecting statements too often; however, as this can make it look like you do not actually understand the other person. Using them once in a while validates the other person. Using them consistently makes it seem as though you are asking the other person to validate your understanding which can lead to them questioning if you are even listening,to begin with.

Ask Them Questions

After you have made a reflecting statement, ask the other person a question. This is a great way to begin directing the conversation and supporting them in communicating in a more clear manner. Ask them if they can elaborate on how they are feeling or what has gotten them to this point. That is a great way to encourage productive dialogue that can support you in better understanding the other person. Then, you can communicate effectively in a way that supports them in better understanding you, too.

Asking questions is a great way to begin diffusing any situation that may be emotionally charged. When you ask questions, you encourage the person to begin sharing and you essentially guide them through a productive conversation. As a result, they begin to feel like you genuinely care and their emotional needs begin to feel accommodated for. Then, you can engage in the conversation in a way that supports your emotional needs and also being met too. In most cases, asking plenty of questions and encouraging the other person to share and support you in understanding can diminish the emotional intensity of any situation.

One big reason as to why asking questions helps is because it pushes the person to begin thinking about answers. As this happens, it encourages their rational mind to come back into perspective. Slowly, they are able to start considering things with greater rationality until they are able to reason their way through the conversation. This can bring them back from an emotional hijacking and lead to them feeling more confident and in charge of their emotions during the conversation.

Bring Movement into the Conversation

If a person does not seem to be calming down, a great way to begin diffusing a situation is to start moving around and walking. Emotions bring up a great deal of energy in people and this energy, if unused, can become destructive and disruptive. Instead of being used physically, it can be expressed through their emotional expression. This can lead to a person expressing themselves in an extremely volatile way merely because the energy within them from their emotions is too intense.

Inviting the person to walk with you and then moving around for a bit is a great way to begin moving that energy out of them so that they can calm down. Climbing up a few flights of stairs, walking around the building, or even just changing which room you are sitting in can be a great way to ease people's emotions. When you begin moving around or encouraging the person to do something else this results with the physiological demands that are being placed on the brain, to change. As a result, they are able to "snap out" of intense emotional experiences and begin feeling more present at the moment. This can support them in bringing back their rational thinking and working towards a solution with you.

Encourage Them to Share Their Perspective

Often, people's emotions will escalate if they feel misunderstood or ignored. If you are not taking the time to understand the other person and their perspective, they can begin to feel as though you do not actually care. This can lead to them feeling as though they need to fight even harder to be heard and understood. As a result, their emotions can escalate as they attempt to get this need to be heard and understood fulfilled.

Rather than waiting for the other person to grow angry and fight harder to be heard, ask them to share their perspective. Taking some time to listen to their side of the story and to understand their feelings is a great way to begin understanding where they are coming from. It also shows a great deal of respect and consideration toward the other person which encourages them to stay calm and continue expressing themselves.

As they are sharing their story, listen to see if you can understand where the primary problems began to present themselves. Pay attention to how that person felt deep down or how they didn't get what they expected or wanted. If you are in doubt about anything, ask them to clarify for you. This is going to help them feel better but it is also going to help you get a clearer idea on what is going on. As a result, you can approach the situation with a greater consideration toward the other person.

Identify What Matters to Them

As you learned earlier in this chapter, people generally become emotionally charged because they feel that something they value has been violated. Learning what this person values and what matters to them right now at this moment can be very helpful in navigating emotionally charged situations.

The best way to discover what the person values and what matters most to them,is to ask them what they wanted and why they wanted it. This supports you in understanding what they were looking for and why it mattered so much to them. As a result, you can understand what their values are. You can also consider what they are looking for right now at this moment which supports you in understanding what matters to them in the present. Typically, their present concerns somehow correlate to their overall values.

After you have learned what someone's values are, there is a wonderful opportunity to use a reflection statement. This supports you in reflecting the perceived value back to the other person so that they can confirm that you understand correctly. This, again, supports them in feeling as though they have been heard and understood. As a result, they can start relaxing and trusting that you are actively considering their concern as you both search for a solution.

Once you know what someone else values, you can begin looking for even more ways to diffuse the situation and reach a mutual agreement. This way, both of you feel as though your needs are being accommodated for and you are able to feel satisfied with the resolution.

Excuse Yourself from the Conversation

If you are having a conversation with someone and it is emotionally charged and does not seem to be relaxing no matter what you do, you are certainly allowed to excuse yourself from the conversation. Excusing yourself from a conversation if you need to, shows that you are not going to let someone else's emotions impact your own emotions. It also shows that you are not willing to let someone else treat you poorly because they are struggling with their emotions.

When people become too emotional, sometimes their brain becomes flooded with emotions and they truly cannot resume a state of rational thinking. This results because their brain begins creating several chemicals that are meant to induce a state of fight or flight. Once this process becomes too advanced, they may not be able to slow it down or stop it. When this happens, sometimes it can take up to 48 hours for the chemicals to completely wear off.

If you are struggling to have a rational and reasonable conversation with someone else, do not make it about them and their emotions. Instead, make it about you. Make the decision to end the conversation and maintain your own emotional well-being in the meantime. Simply let them know that you have a prior commitment that you need to keep and that you need to excuse yourself. Let them know that you are more than happy to talk about the conversation again in the future but that, in the meantime, you need to leave. This gives both of you plenty of time to calm down so that you can approach the subject once again from a more rational perspective.

Apologize If You Need To

If at any point you find out that you did something that leads to the other person's emotional response, always make sure that you apologize. Even if they also need to apologize for how they behaved in accordance with their emotions, make sure that you apologize too. It doesn't matter if you intended to say what you did or if you didn't, if you created pain in someone else, always apologize.

Being able to take responsibility for your own contribution to someone else's emotions is important. This shows that you are emotionally mature enough that you can recognize how you contributed to someone else's feelings becoming hurt and that you are not going to try to pass the blame or use excuses to bypass what you did. Instead, you are willing to accept that you did something that hurt someone else and, if need be, you will help find a solution to rectify those hurt feelings.

Chapter 8: Using Your EQ to Build Healthy Relationships

One of the biggest reasons why EQ is so important is because it has such a massive impact on your ability to have healthy relationships with other people. Using your EQ to develop and maintain healthy relationships with others can support you in having more positive experiences with those in your life. This makes you more enjoyable for others to be around and makes your relationships more enjoyable for you too.

If you have ever suffered from toxic emotions in relationships, then you understand how frustrating and damaging they truly can be. Toxic emotions can quickly turn into a toxic relationship that results in both parties consistently feeling as though they are being left in a negative state after your shared interactions. Using your EQ in your relationships can support you in eliminating toxic emotional damage. It can also support you in cultivating new friendships and relationships with other people who also seek to express themselves in a more productive and healthy manner. As a result, you can begin developing stronger and healthier relationships through your higher EQ.

Building Healthy Relationships Feels Good

Humans are naturally drawn towards being social. Even though there are some people who are more social than others, we all have an equal need to have some form of social structure in our lives. Being a part of a community matters to us and joining in with those around us feels good. However, when we are not taught to behave in a way that supports us in having healthy connections with those around us, it can be painful.

Toxic relationships rarely stem on purpose. Instead, it often happens because we are not taught how to socialize properly. As a result, we are unable to "fit in" with healthier relationships. Instead, we end up building relationships with other people who, like us, also don't know how to socialize properly. The result is that two people who do not know how to communicate are then left in a relationship where they both continually have emotional outbursts. Since neither party knows how to effectively identify and express their emotions, both parties end up expressing themselves in poor manners. Often, the toxicity that results in these relationships is not on purpose. Instead, it is simply caused by a lack of knowledge.

These toxic outbursts and interactions result in people feeling as though socializing is a negative behavior. Since this directly contradicts the needs of every human, it can result in a significant emotional backlash. Feelings of being unworthy, incapable, unwanted and unloved can surface in each individual. This can result in poor emotional health which can lead to mental illness over time. What ends up happening is that both parties are directly and indirectly negatively impacted by the unhealthy relationship.

Learning how to build healthy relationships supports you in having positive interactions with those around you. As a result, the positive attention you receive feels good. This also stimulates your natural human need to be a part of a community. Because you are both receiving the social interaction that you need and receiving positive attention, your emotions begin to feel even better. This can actually lead to even healthier emotional expression over time as you begin feeling more confident in understanding and expressing yourself.

This means that learning how to use your EQ to build healthier relationships is actually going to help you feel significantly better in your life. Any emotional challenges that you presently face as a result of toxic emotional interactions with others will begin to diminish. Over time, you will discover that interacting with others actually feels good. Your natural need to socialize will also be fulfilled, leaving you feeling satisfied after social encounters. This will promote a healthy emotional, psychological, and social wellbeing in your life. As a result, you will feel better overall.

Influencing Your Relationships with EQ

Building healthy relationships using your EQ requires you to spend time truly investing in understanding yourself. Taking the time to grow self-aware is going to support you in recognizing what your emotional self is like. This self-awareness and self-understanding are going to support you in discovering how you tend to behave in social interactions.

As this understanding develops within you, you can begin to think rationally about how you behave in social interactions. Your understanding around who you are, how you tend to engage in these interactions, and what you need grows. It becomes easier for you to discover how you are feeling, why, and what you need to do in order to manage these feelings. This means that you will have more control over yourself in social settings even when your emotions are being triggered.

Your ability to effectively understand and control your emotions is also going to improve your ability to communicate with other people. Through this ability, you can communicate in a way that is clear and concise. You can also exercise empathy and compassion in your conversations. This ensures that you are both sending a clear message whenever you speak *and* understanding the messages being sent back to you.

When your communication improves and when it is particularly void of toxic negative emotional expressions, your ability to connect with others is improved. You are able to consider other people, understand them on an emotional level, and have compassion for them in a way that others might not. This improves your closeness and supports you both in sharing a positive relationship.

It is important to recognize that in any relationship, you are going to have some form of disagreement. They always happen. Furthermore, you might have times where one or both of you intend to spend time together but you are in a bad mood from something that happened earlier that day. Knowing how to handle your emotions and manage other people's emotions can ensure that these types of experiences remain calm and effective. Instead of any bad moods or disagreements leading to an emotionally charged argument, they can be resolved. Both of you can feel as though your needs have been met and then you can move forward with a clean slate of healthy emotions.

Becoming a More Supportive Friend

The ability to understand emotions on a more intimate level means that you have the capacity to become a supportive friend to the people in your life. When you know how to understand emotions in yourself and in others and how to manage other people's emotions, this supports you in being more empathetic. When you are more empathetic, it is easier for you to be compassionate towards other people.

Empathy supports you in genuinely understanding the needs and concerns of other people. This means that you don't only hear the needs and concerns but you genuinely feel the importance and urgency of these feelings in the other person. You can then express yourself in a way that actually shows your compassion and concern for the other person. This helps them to realize that they truly are being understood. Then, they end up feeling supported by you.

Your ability to express empathy and compassion for your friends is not the only way that you can show them support either. When you share a positive relationship with other people, you also share positive attention. This means that anytime you are around each other, you will feel more positive. As a result, the very act of coming together feels supportive and uplifting. You both trust that you can confide in the other person and receive support if it is needed, so you end up feeling supported just by each other's presence. This makes your friendship even more valuable to each of you.

Learning How to Contribute to Positive Emotions

Knowing how to manage your emotions means that you can intentionally contribute to a relationship with more positive emotions. When you do not know how to manage your emotions, you have a tendency to carry a lot of stress and pessimism around with you. This means that even if you don't mean to, your interactions with other people can be filled with negativity and pessimism. You find yourself complaining excessively, feeling frustrated and angry, and struggling to experience any joy. For others, this can feel like you are constantly in a bad mood. This makes you less of a joy to be around. In fact, they may actually find themselves feeling worse after hanging out with you.

Naturally, you do not want to bring negativity and pessimism into anyone's life. You don't want this for yourself or for anyone that you care about. Learning how to improve your EQ means that your general stress levels are reduced. As a result, you are less likely to carry this pessimism and negativity around with you. Furthermore, on days where you are feeling particularly stressed out, you can express it productively. This means that you may share a conversation about why you are stressed but then you will set the stress aside and go on to enjoy yourself.

Knowing how to manage your emotions is an excellent way

to begin sharing more positive contributions to your relationships. This can support you in sharing good memories and both increasing each other's good vibes as you hang out. As a result, people will leave your time together feeling more positive and uplifted. This is a far more positive and enjoyable experience than if you were not able to manage your emotions effectively!

Chapter 9: Applying EQ in the Real World

Throughout this book, you have been offered many examples as to how a high EQ can impact your life. However, you may still be wondering how your EQ truly can be applied in the real world. The reality is, relationships and careers are a big part of our lives but they are not the only parts of our lives. There are many moving parts in our lives that contribute to our overall sense of wellbeing.

Knowing how to manage your emotions is not only going to improve your relationships and career. It is also going to support you in having a better life in general. In this chapter, we are going to show you how you truly can apply your higher EQ to life in general. This way, you can discover the many other areas of your life where your EQ can improve your general sense of wellbeing.

Developing a Stronger Sense of Self

One of the key elements of developing your EQ is developing your sense of self. As you begin to put in the work to understand your emotions and your needs, your relationship with yourself begins to evolve. Through your practice and efforts, you need results. From those results, you begin to prove to yourself that you have what it takes to get your needs met. As a result, your general sense of well-being improves. So, too, does your confidence and your self-esteem.

You begin trusting that you know how to get your needs met, so meeting your needs becomes a lot easier. You also trust that you know how to navigate emotionally charged situations in a way that does not create a negative backlash. As a result, you become more confident in navigating these situations. This is true even for the more challenging ones such as confrontations.

The more you continue to explore yourself and understand your emotions, the more you have the opportunity to heal. The things that once ailed you such as painful memories and emotional triggers begin to subside. You develop the ability to overcome these things and release them once and for all. As a result, you can actually heal emotional traumas that have burdened you for many years.

Expanding on your emotional intelligence will also support you in feeling confident in being able to create the life that you desire. Your deeper understanding of yourself supports you in knowing what it is that will result in you getting or having what you want. This means that you will have an easier time having your needs actually met. As a result, your sense of self and relationship with yourself will grow even more.

Having Healthier Engagements with Strangers

Having a stronger EQ will actually make your engagements with strangers healthier and more productive. We often don't think of our cngagements with people we don't know to be uncomfortable or awkward, but they can be. When we have engagements with strangers, we are speaking with people that we do not already know. This means that we have no preconceived idea as to who they are, what they are typically like, or how they process their emotions. In many cases, this can lead to awkward and uncomfortable interactions.

For example, say you are at the store purchasing something new. As you are, the person whom you are purchasing your new item through seems grumpy and frustrated. If you did not have a high EQ, you might match their emotions. As a result, your exciting new item may be tarnished by the feelings of being frustrated because you met the sales person's energy. If you had a higher EQ, however, you might actually be able to change the engagement. Through your ability to manage other people's emotions, you could begin joking and speaking in a way that they respond to with greater positivity. As a result, your own purchasing experience is enjoyable. Furthermore, you may even improve the overall mood of the salesperson. If you were unable to improve their mood, at the very least you could prevent it from impacting your own.

We interact with many people on a daily basis. Some of these people are positive, some of them are not so positive. Knowing how to manage your own emotions can result in you not having such a strong negative reaction every time someone else does. This can support you in either having more positive experiences or at least more neutral experiences. This way, you do not carry the weight of the world with you everywhere that you go.

Asking for Help More Effectively

When you work towards improving your EQ, you also improve your capacity to ask for help. Knowing how to ask for help and receive help is important but many people do not actually know how. It may seem silly to consider since asking for help is as simple as asking a question. However, many people do not know how to ask for help or they simply don't ask for help for many reasons.

People who do not know how to ask for help often find themselves not knowing how because they don't know what they actually need. As a result, they don't actually know what to ask for. This leads to them feeling frustrated because they know that they have a need but they do not know what that need is. This result in them not knowing how to actually get that need met. So, the need goes unmet and their frustration grows. The longer the need is unmet, the higher their frustrations get, and the harder it is for them to identify it and ask.

Another reason why people don't ask for help is that they are afraid of being judged. Their fear of judgment leads to them being too guilty or ashamed to ask for the help they need. They worry that if they were to ask, they would not receive the help they need. Furthermore, they may actually instead receive ridicule and judgment. This leads to people being afraid of asking for help because they don't want their needs, which matter to them, being treated as invalid or ridiculous.

When you learn how to both identify your emotions and express them in a way that you can get your needs met, it becomes a lot easier for you to ask for help. It also becomes easier for you to ask in a way that other people are willingly interested in helping you. This can lead to you receiving greater results from asking which means that you become even more confident in the process. As you continue to have positive results from asking for help such as getting your needs met, it becomes even easier to ask. Before you know it, asking to have your needs met is simple and your needs are always met because you are asking. It is a win-win situation!

Actually Receiving Positive Solutions

When you know how to ask to have your needs met in a way that is kind and polite towards others, what ends up happening is that you begin receiving more positive solutions. This leads to a greater confidence in asking, but it also leads to a greater sense of fulfillment.

Think about it, when someone asks you for help in a way that is polite and sincere, you are likely going to want to help them. In fact, you may even go above and beyond because you are genuinely interested in helping this person. Alternatively, if someone asks you for help but is ignorant or impolite about it, you might help. If you do, however, that help will likely be offered in a way that is the bare minimum. In fact, you may even cut corners and not fully help them because you just want to end the exchange.

When you learn how to incorporate your EQ into your ability to ask for help, people are going to offer you more positive solutions. You may find yourself getting even more than you bargained for because you were polite and pleasant to deal with. As a result, you end up feeling even more satisfied because your needs are completely met *and then some*. Plus, you got them met without having to engage in a negative interaction first. Because the experience was more pleasurable and enjoyable from start to finish, it was easier to feel truly satisfied with the results you were given. This will make asking for help and trusting that you will have your needs meteven easier, further establishing your confidence in yourself and in others.

Having a Healthier Network

The more you practice developing your EQ, the more you are going to begin attracting people into your life who also have a higher EQ. People always prefer to connect with those who they are similar to. Furthermore, those with a higher EQ have a tendency to demand higher levels of respect and compassion from those in their lives. Knowing how to offer this to others means that you are also going to expect the same in return.

As you grow more accustomed to offering and receiving this level of respect and compassion from others, you will find that you look for this quality more in others. Furthermore, you will actually attract others who look for this quality in their network too. As a result, your entire network of friends and associates will grow to reflect that of one that is filled with individuals with a high EQ.

A healthier network is one that is far more fulfilling. Rather than having friends and acquaintances that you avoid or that you have resentment towards, you will have people in your network that you genuinely enjoy engaging with. As a result, you will be more likely to want to engage with them. This makes going out and fulfilling your social needs more enjoyable. It also means that you will have a network of people that you can genuinely rely on and trust in.

The more you begin developing your EQ, the more you might find yourself shifting your social circle. Networking with people who do not focus on self-development may begin to lose its appeal for you as you no longer communicate or express yourself in the same way that they do. As a result, communicating with them can feel strained and uncomfortable. This is why most people who embark on self-development journeys change who they hang out with the most. We all prefer to spend time around people who genuinely reflect our values and whom we can relate to. You will likely find yourself making this adjustment over time too.

Learning How to Fully Forgive and Move On

Part of what keeps people in a chronic state of stress is holding on to painful experiences that they had in the past. Not knowing how to truly forgive and heal from painful experiences that you have had can lead to you feeling as though you are being held hostage by them. You may find yourself holding grudges, experiencing painful flashbacks, and struggling with many painful emotional triggers. The amount of emotional backlash that you can experience as a result of not knowing how to fully forgive people and heal from painful experiences is massive.

As you begin to develop your EQ, you will find that forgiving people becomes a lot easier. This is not because the pain becomes any less painful but because you learn how to actually process the pain and then fully release it. You begin to realize that holding onto pain and bottling it up inside only hurts you and the only way around that is to feel it and release it.

Another reason why forgiveness becomes easier is that you discover that it is a lot harder to hold a grudge when you can experience empathy for the other person. When you are able to stop and consider their perspective and understand where they come from, as well as take responsibility for your own contributions, it is harder to stay angry. Instead, your rational mind begins to come into play and seeks to mentally process the experiences that happened to you.

For many people, EQ is a powerful way to overcome traumas and painful experiences that they have been holding onto throughout their life. As you continue to develop your own, you will likely find that you naturally start working through forgiveness and healing in your self-reflection. As a result, your residual stress and negative feelings will begin to diminish as your emotional bottle begins to empty itself out.

Reducing the Amount of Judgment You Pass

When we cannot fully experience and express empathy, we also cannot fully understand and accept others. People with a low EQ have a tendency to be very judgmental towards other people. Nearly everything is a reason for others to be judged when you lack a strong EQ. However, these changes as you begin to develop your emotional management.

The more you develop your EQ, the more empathetic you begin to feel towards others. In addition to empathizing with them emotionally, you also begin to empathize with their perspective and the life they may live. As a result, you realize that there is truly no reason to judge them. So, you become more accepting.

As you become more accepting towards others, many things in your life begin to change. You begin to realize that people make mistakes and that mistakes are human. So, forgiveness becomes easier. You also begin to realize that not everything is black and white, so you have an easier time understanding when people do things that don't make sense to you. This means that even if you don't agree with the other person, you can still respect them and their decisions.

Lastly and perhaps most importantly, is the ability to be more accepting. It means that you are able to make more relationships with better people. When you are able to accept others as they are and refrain from judging them, you often realize that virtually everyone has something valuable to offer to the world around them. As a result, you begin to establish more friendships and connections with people that you may have never considered previously. This is because you are no longer judging them over smaller things that do not truly matter. Instead, you are taking the time to genuinely get to know them and understand them.

This contributes to your social network growing. It also supports you in your ability to learn something from everyone that you meet.

Discovering Ways That You Can Continue Learning

In life, we are constantly learning. Each day we truly do learn something new. When you develop your EQ, you realize this very knowledge. People who lack a strong EQ are known to become arrogant and complacent. They may believe that they know everything they need to know so there is nothing left to learn. Or, they may feel that they know enough and so they never evolve who they are or how they approach life. As a result, you end up with people who are "stuck in their ways" with "ways" that are ineffective and unproductive. You might watch them have negative experiences time and again only to hear them repeatedly chalk it up to "you can't teach old dog new tricks." The truth is they simply lack the understanding of what it takes to learn and grow.

People who have a strong EQ understand that life never stops changing. Every day you learn something new, things change, and society shifts just a little bit more. Equipped with this understanding, you can maintain an open mind so that you can continue learning and adapt to these ever-changing ways. In the end, you end up finding yourself growing and evolving easier than ever before.

A great way to begin reaping in the benefits of your EQ is using your emotional understanding to support you in learning. Use your understanding to help you practice delaying your gratification so that you can commit to learning even more. This will support you in increasing your self-development. It will also support you in developing the skills that you need to achieve the goals that you have set for yourself in life. The more you practice learning, the further you can get in life. You should always work towards learning, and your EQ will support you in learning even more and with greater success.

Chapter 10: Embracing Your Emotional Journey

As you continue to proceed down the path of mastering your emotional intelligence, there is plenty that is to be learned. As we mentioned in chapter 9, you can always learn more. There truly is no cap for learning. This means that your emotional journey will be a life-long journey that you need to embrace.

Learning how to embrace this journey takes time, practice, and daily devotion. In this chapter, we are going to show you how you can embrace your emotional journey fully so that you can continue evolving your EQ. The more you continue practicing these efforts, the easier it is going to be for you to continue doing so. However, that does not mean that it will *always* be easy. Still, your commitment to yourself can be.

Realize That You Are Not Perfect

It is imperative that you never see yourself as a perfect human, no matter how compelling the idea may be. Placing the pressure of being perfect on yourself means that you take away from your right to make mistakes. This can have serious negative repercussions on your overall wellbeing.

As you continue to embrace your emotional journey going forward, make sure that you stay realistic about who you are and what you can reasonably do. If you make a mistake, do not bully yourself or beat yourself up over that. Instead, recognize that this is a wonderful opportunity for you to reflect and grow. That way, you always use every mistake as a lesson to support you in doing better going forward.

When you hold realistic expectations over yourself and what you can reasonably achieve, it also ensures that you do not place too much pressure on yourself right off of the start. If you have never known how to express yourself in a positive manner, there is certainly no way that you will achieve this overnight. Accepting this means that you can place reasonable expectations on yourself and hold yourself to these more reasonable standards rather than trying to achieve everything all at once. As a result, you will find it much easier for you to continue moving forward since you are supporting yourself and your ability to succeed.

Continue Practicing Every Single Day

No matter how you are feeling and no matter how short you might be on time, always ensure that you invest in your emotional development every single day. Even if you can only commit to five minutes of self-reflection that evening and the rest of the day was filled with mistakes, do it. The more you commit, the easier it is to stay committed and continue developing.

Staying committed is much easier when you stay realistic with yourself, too. So, using the aforementioned point of being patient with yourself will support you in your commitment. Never use a mistake or a setback as a reason to break your commitment or stop your practice. The minute you do, you are the one that suffers. You need to commit to practicing in some way, even if it is only a small way, at least once every single day.

Early on, it might be helpful for you to have an accountability partner or set up some form of system to support you in staying committed. Having a reminder system and then using rewards to celebrate your commitment may support you in actually staying committed. As your commitment to yourself and your development becomes easier, you can start moving toward using your own reward system as a way to further boost your EQ. An exampleis delaying your rewards a few days or weeks at a time but making each reward larger. This will not only keep you committed but will also support you in further developing your practice.

Embrace Each Emotion Equally

As much as you might not want to, it is essential that you commit to embracing each emotion equally. Refrain from judging your emotions and avoiding emotions that you consider to be negative or unpleasant. This can result in you bottling up your negative or more painful emotions and later expressing them in an unhealthy and toxic manner.

Whenever you experience an emotion, no matter how intense or how painful it might be, give yourself the space that you need to embrace that emotion. If it is particularly intense and challenging, consider expressing it privately before expressing it to another person. This can ensure that you work through the emotion, understand it, and get your management in check before you begin expressing yourself to someone else. Then, when you are ready to tell the other person, you are already somewhat diffused on your own so the sharing process is a lot easier.

As you begin to learn how to process all of your emotions and embrace each of them equally, you will start to discover that emotions are not necessarily a bad thing. Instead, it is often the way that we experience and express them that turns them into a negative experience. Anger, for example, can be incredibly fueling and productive. Unless we express it in a way that results in some form of negative backlash, then, anger becomes negative and toxic. The more you practice, the more likely you will be to have your emotions always serve you in one way or another. As a result, you will learn to respect and express each of them equally and with appreciation and understanding toward all of them.

Develop a Mindfulness Practice

When you are developing your EQ, spending time developing a mindfulness practice is also a powerful thing to do. Mindfulness practices including meditation and yoga are a wonderful way to begin drawing your attention into your body. The entire point of these practices is to support you in getting to know yourself on a deeper and more intimate level. They improve your self-awareness and support you in understanding yourself with deeper intensity.

As you develop your mindfulness practice, this insight into yourself will support you in understanding your own emotions. It will also support you in healing and processing the emotions that have remained bottled up within you all of this time. As a result, you will find that your natural state begins to grow more and more content. Rather than carrying stress around on your shoulders non-stop, you will find yourself carrying around peace and satisfaction.

A strong mindfulness practice can be a great asset for anyone seeking to develop their EQ. There are many great resources that you can tap into to discover how you can begin developing your mindfulness practice right away. For example, meditating, yoga, and breath work are all great practices to help you develop a mindfulness practice. We strongly recommend you do so if you want to truly master the art of having a strong EQ.

Slow Down When You Need To

One thing that is essential when it comes to looking after your emotional health is recognizing the importance of slowing down when you need to. Far too often, we feel as though we must continue working and pushing ourselves even when we are feeling stressed out. This leads to even greater levels of stress which are extremely hard to overcome. In the end, we struggle to manage even smaller stressors because we are feeling emotionally overwhelmed.

When you feel as though your emotions are starting to become overwhelmed or you are experiencing strong emotions, it is imperative that you learn to give yourself permission to slow down. Acknowledging your emotions and giving yourself adequate time and space to manage and heal them can support you in feeling better in the end. The sooner you process and heal big emotions, the sooner you can move forward without feeling overworked. Emotions that are left unacknowledged or unprocessed always lead to a weakened ability to manage emotions in the long run.

Sometimes, simply acknowledging an emotion is not enough. Emotions that are felt in extreme ways need more time and attention to process. Make sure that you give yourself the time that is needed to support you in overcoming these emotions. In the end, you will find it much easier to increase your ability to manage your emotions when you are also giving yourself plenty of time to process them and keep your emotional tank "clean."

Studies have shown that people who take one day per week to completely rest are actually significantly healthier than others. Their emotional and mental health is significantly increased when people regularly take the time to slow down and rest. Giving yourself just one day to take it easy, let go of chores and to-do lists and enjoy life can have incredible benefits on your overall health.

Conclusion

Congratulations on completing the book *"Emotional Intelligence Mastery (EQ):* The Guide to Mastering Emotions and Why It Can Matter More Than IQ!"

This book was designed to support you in understanding the value of EQ and how you can begin mastering it in your own life. We hope that in reading this book you were able to better understand how your emotional health and management can impact your life. Through effective management, you stand to gain many massive and empowering benefits from improving your EQ.

We also hope that in reading this book you were able to have a better understanding of how your emotions work and how they impact you in your life. Realizing the sheer power of emotions can support you in recognizing the importance of your emotions and giving this work the time and attention it requires. This will support you in staying motivated to continue applying the many practical practices that you were shown in this book. Through practical application, everything is learned and integrated with greater success. This will make it significantly easier for you to begin mastering your EQ sooner.

As you move forward through this book, make sure that you are remembering the importance of embracing your emotional journey. Remember, as a human, you are driven by two core "centers": your emotions and your reason. Because of this, sometimes you might find yourself being more driven by your emotions than your reason. When this begins, you want to give yourself time to process the emotions that are causing such an intense reaction. This will ensure that you are able to process them effectively and restore your ability to think clearly and resume rational thinking processes.

If you are someone who has struggled with your emotions for a long time, you might find that having support will be helpful in you managing and overcoming your emotions. This will ensure that you are not attempting to face challenging and potentially overwhelming emotions alone. Knowing how and when to ask for help is imperative to your wellbeing. Emotions can be challenging and knowing how to seek and receive support can be life-changing.

When you are done reading this book, it is important that you do not simply stop your practice. Emotional mastery is something that you can continually improve in. Maintain your daily self-reflection and check-ins and make sure that you are constantly looking for new ways to improve. Remember, you can never be done learning. There is always more to know. Furthermore, you are always growing your emotional self and needs are always changing too. Giving yourself what you need in every moment and taking the time to recognize what that is will support you in your true self-mastery.

Lastly, if you enjoyed *"Emotional Intelligence Mastery (EQ):* The Guide to Mastering Emotions and Why It Can Matter More Than IQ", we ask that you please take the time to honestly review it. Your feedback would be greatly appreciated.

Thank you!

www.ingramcontent.com/pod-product-compliance
Lightning Source LLC
Chambersburg PA
CBHW071238070526
44583CB00017B/2236